Notebook Know-How

Notebook Know-How
Strategies for the Writer's Notebook

Aimee Buckner

Foreword by Ralph Fletcher

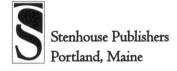

Stenhouse Publishers
Portland, Maine

Stenhouse Publishers
www.stenhouse.com

Credits

"Call the Periods Call the Commas" reprinted with the permission of Simon & Schuster Books for Young Readers, an imprint of Simon & Schuster Children's Publishing Division from *If You're Not Here, Please Raise Your Hand* by Kalli Dakos. Text copyright © 1990 Kalli Dakos.

Excerpt from *John Henry* by Julius Lester, copyright © 1994 by Julius Lester. Used by permission of Dial Books for Young Readers, a Division of Penguin Young Readers Group, a Member of Penguin Group (USA) Inc., 345 Hudson Street, New York, NY 10014. All Rights reserved.

Library of Congress Cataloging-in-Publication Data

Buckner, Aimee E. (Aimee Elizabeth), 1970-
    Notebook know how : strategies for the writer's notebook.
        p. cm.
    Includes bibliographical references.
    ISBN 1-57110-413-5
        1. English language—Composition and exercises—Study and teaching (Elementary) 2. Language arts (Elementary) 3. Creative writing (Elementary education) 4. Notebooks. I. Title.

LB1576.B883 2005
372.62'3—dc22

2005042563

Cover and interior design by Beth Caissie

Manufactured in the United States of America on acid-free paper
15 14 13 12 11 10   15 14 13 12 11 10

Dedication

For Judith Eggemeier and Nina MacKellar—
A small tribute to your grand influence

Table of Contents

Figures List

Foreword

At certain times in my life I have found myself believing that being an outstanding teacher is one of those things you're either born with, or you're not. At other times I've realized that, to the contrary, highly skilled teaching is something you can acquire through hard work. But maybe it's a combination of the two. On a few rare occasions I've encountered a born teacher who has worked very hard to develop her considerable skills into an art.

I first met Aimee Buckner ten years ago, and quickly realized that she had a great deal to offer. She struck me as a teacher who would one day make a significant contribution to our field.

"Aimee's got a good book in her," I boldly predicted to Philippa Stratton, the Editorial Director at Stenhouse. "At *least* one book."

What made me say that? On several occasions I had the good fortune to visit Aimee's fourth grade classroom, and I was struck by the palpable seriousness in that classroom. Her kids were still kids, but they weren't fooling around when they got down to their writing. They wrote with voice, and you couldn't miss how much they cared about their writing.

Later Aimee mailed me samples of her students' notebook entries and finished drafts. Amazing stuff! Even though I am a process-oriented person, I have always believed that student writing is a strong predictor of what a teacher is doing with her students in any classroom. From the quality of the writing—the voice, the energy, the undeniable investment students showed in their work—I knew that Aimee Buckner was the kind of teacher that I, as a parent, would want for my own children.

In 1996 my wife JoAnn Portalupi planned a summer institute in Birmingham, Alabama. The institute would include demonstration classes of student writers, and I suggested that JoAnn bring in Aimee Buckner to work with the middle school kids. Teaching middle school kids during a summer school session could have been a daunting task, but under Aimee's guidance they wrote with conviction and with voice. "There's something magical happening in that class," JoAnn told me after the first week of that institute.

In writing my own books for young writers, I have been indebted to a small group of outstanding teachers who have sent me samples of their students' writing. Pieces from Aimee's students show up in every one of these books. Whenever I received a packet from Aimee, I opened it with a great deal of excitement but also guilt. Although I was thrilled to use these writing samples, I always had a nagging voice in my head that said, "Eventually, Aimee Buckner must incorporate such lovely student writing into a book of her own."

And this is what she has done. Every teacher educator must find a place from which to speak. Lucy Calkins speaks from the vantage point of the Teachers College Reading and Writing Project and the New York City schools. In the tradition of Donald Murray, I have used my own writing as a reference point for most of my professional books. Aimee's writing is grounded in her careful, thoughtful teaching. This book is richly seasoned with stories, profiles of kids, and anecdotes drawn from years of teaching experience. In this book the reader finds him or herself in the hands of a sure teacher. There is a sense of authority that permeates every sentence of every page.

Aimee's subject, helping students keep a writer's notebook, is one that I have tried to tackle in two of my own books. While I have approached this topic from a writer's perspective, Aimee explores it from a teacher's point of view. The notebook can be a powerful tool for student writers, but how does a teacher make the notebook tangible and useful for young writers? Where do you go once the notebook has been launched? How do you get it humming in the classroom?

Aimee deals with a wealth of practical issues and predictable problems including getting started, organizing the notebook, assessment, and a great deal more. We get to eavesdrop on actual lessons and writing conferences. Most important, we get to hear the thinking that underlies every decision she makes in her teaching. This is a very wise book—again and again I found myself nodding as the author illuminated an idea that I had not completely articulated to myself. And while it is enormously practical, readers will appreciate the fact that it is appropriately leavened by warmth and humor.

You know what I appreciated most while reading it? This book is a throwback. How refreshing to read a book about teaching writing in 2005 that doesn't apologize for its subject, that doesn't feel obliged to disguise it as something trendy and contemporary such as curriculum, or standards, or test preparation. Reading this book, I felt my old passions rekindled, and remembered what drew me to this field in the first place. That's the best kind of teacher renewal I can imagine.

Ralph Fletcher

Acknowledgments

Teaching can be a lonely job. There are days I don't even see the teachers who teach next door to me or across the hall. It is easy to fall prey to isolation. I have had the blessing of working with people who have fought this isolation as much as I have. Without them, I wouldn't have questioned, researched, or reflected on my teaching as much as I do today. Without them, this book would be empty.

Thank you, Rhonda Mumaw. You took me under your wing in the early days and showed me what it means to truly teach. Thanks to the staff at Brookwood Elementary School in Gwinnett County, Georgia. You are all models of lifelong learners, and I am proud to teach among you. And to Maxine Rithmire, fearless leader of Brookwood Elementary, a true visionary in education. Please don't ever retire.

I'd also like to thank the teachers at the Gwinnett County Summer Writing Institute. Over the past seven years, I have had the opportunity to work with some of the best teachers I have ever met. I learn from you each year and am so thankful for your tireless efforts to help other teachers find their way. These teachers include Georgia Tomlin, Jolinda Collins, Patrick Norton, Martha Finnegan, Fern LeMaster, Charlie Hollingshead, Dean Looney, Kim Looney, Kathy McKinzey, Adam Crawley, Pam Wallace, Debbie Rizk, Bobbie Williams, Carla Stanford, Cheryl Cole, and Clayborn Knight. Also, thank you, Joyce Berube, for your continual efforts to keep the institute well funded.

I have had mentors over the years. Some have known it and some have not. They are the authors of books about teaching; the people around the country who drew me into their classroom with their stories and ideas. Special thanks to Ralph Fletcher, author, consultant, mentor, and friend. It is your work that has led me here. I hope this book makes you proud. Thank you, Stephanie Harvey, for your insights and encouragement. Your friendship means a lot to me.

Thank you, Christy Malko, for your friendship and professional insight. You kept the assessment question alive until we thought we got it right. And to new friends and colleagues Jeff Anderson and Bruce Morgan. Your energy is intoxicating. I need people like you in my life.

Writing a book is even lonelier than teaching at times. I appreciate my sisters and brother, Chiara, Chantel, and Adam DiMuzio. Your high expectations keep me reaching for the stars. I also want to thank my mom and dad, Christine and William DiMuzio; my colleague Saralyn Wolf; and my friend Catherine Pimental. Your encouragement, willingness to read drafts, and commitment to caring for Mikey as I needed to write has made this endeavor possible. Words are not enough ...

My family read my drafts with the instructions: no criticism, praise only. Margie Forbes, Suzy Kaback, Mary McMackin, and Franki Sibberson, however, read with a critical eye and presented revision suggestions that helped the ideas in this book grow. I appreciate your candor, insight, and valuable help throughout this process.

A big thank-you to Brenda Power. You allowed me to write without much pressure—until the very end, when I needed a push or two. I appreciate that you put up with my quirks, including how you would refer to the book in progress. You are one of the smartest people I know, and it has been my honor to work with you.

As a teacher, I know the pain of editing work. Thank you, Anne Sauvé, for your sharp eye and vast knowledge of grammar. Your help finding even the smallest glitches was priceless. You know what they say (or should say)—behind every good book is a good copyeditor.

Without Jay Kilburn, this book would still be on the computer. Thanks, Jay, for getting the book together in tip-top shape and presenting it in such an elegant manner. You're amazing!

And finally, thanks to all the children who have shared their writing with me whether they wanted to or not. It has been through their efforts that I have seen reflections of my teaching. From them came this book.

Chapter 1:

Why Notebooks?

It was September in Georgia, which means it was *still* hot. My fourth-grade students were filing into the classroom with their first writer's notebooks. The assignment: purchase a notebook that "calls to you"—that yearns for your words to be written down in it. If nothing calls and nothing yearns, then just pick one you like. Everyone must have a notebook for writing today.

As I observed students unpacking this soon-to-be treasure, I noticed that their reactions were as different as the colors in a box of crayons. Some students pulled it out of their backpacks with great drama—carefully taking it out, hugging it close to them, showing their friends, and finally setting it down on top of their desks. Others were much more casual—the notebook was stuck in the middle of a pile of last night's homework and awkwardly shoved in their desks.

Then there was Chance. Chance is a gifted student in all aspects. But he didn't enjoy writing. Although good at it, he saw it as a chore rather than something to enrich and improve his life.

"Where's your notebook?" the girl next to him asked.

"Oh yeah, I almost forgot," he replied while whipping it out of his back pocket. It was a small, pocket-sized spiral notebook, one that is often used for lists or reminders.

"You're going to write in *that*?" she asked, almost as if she were incredulous.

"Well, Ms. B. never said what size. This one caught my eye. I like it. It's small and won't take long to write a whole page. It's perfect."

Then the questions began: How long does an "entry" have to be to count as an assignment? How many of Chance's pages equal one of my pages? Can I get a new notebook like Chance's? How big do the notebooks have to be, Ms. B? I cringed. I hadn't thought about any notebook requirements. I thought the students would … well, they would just *know* what I wanted. The fact is that in the beginning many children will not honor and cherish their notebooks just because I'm excited about them.

Fast-forward several years to another new school year. Two (of several) reasons I love my job are we get to start afresh each school year, and we get to use school supplies. I'm a maniac when it comes to supplies. I love shopping for pencils, markers, notebooks, and glue. Scanning the sales section of the Sunday paper beginning in July is like a challenge on *Survivor!* Can I hold out for the best deal and then grab it before anyone else does?

After my experience with Chance, I decided to purchase all the notebooks and folders required for each student. A local store was having a sale: ten spiral notebooks and folders for a dollar. It was a bargain shopper's dream, never mind a lover of school supplies. So I went in and scoured the boxes of notebooks and folders to color-coordinate subject notebooks with subject folders. As I pulled everything out of the cart for the checkout clerk, she commented, "What do you need all of this for?"

"They're for my kids," I replied without thinking.

With a look of shock mixed with horror she asked, "How many children do you have?!"

Still clueless as to why she would be shocked I said, "Twenty-five."

"Twenty-five children! They can't all be yours!"

I had to laugh as I explained they were my students. The clerk was amazed that I went to all of this trouble for them. I realized then that I was going to a lot of trouble to do too much for them. What else was I doing too much of? The answer came amazingly fast—I did too much of their writing. I said they could write about whatever they wanted, and then I continued to give topics to the students who "have nothing to write about." Instead of showing them how to find topics, I left it up to them to fly solo or I gave them ideas. When I looked at the blank notebooks, my first thought was what am I going to get kids to put in these notebooks?

These inner conversations led me to a deeper study of writer's notebooks. Lucy Calkins and, more recently, Ralph Fletcher have written extensively about notebooks as a tool for prewriting. In *A Writer's Notebook: Unlocking the Writer Within You* (1996a), Fletcher describes notebooks as his most important tool for living a writing kind of life. In *Breathing In, Breathing Out*

(1996b), Fletcher encourages readers: "Don't be afraid to live like a writer. Writers explore. There are two whole universes for you to explore—the one on the inside, and the physical one on the outside. Take your choice; inner or outer. Or best: both" (p. 6).

A writer's notebook gives students a place to write every day ... to practice living like a writer. Anne Lamott's father told her, "Writing ... do it every day for a while. Do it as you would do scales on a piano. Do it by prearrangement with yourself. Do it as a debt of honor and make a commitment to finishing things" (Lamott 1994, p. xxii).

In her book *Something to Declare*, Julia Alvarez says, "The writing life is a life with all the windows and doors opened" (1999, p. 282). That's what notebooks help students do: use the world around them—their own lives and perspectives— as a supply of writing ideas. Don Murray reflects on his notebook as a record of his thinking—a record of his intellectual life. Stephen King, in *On Writing: A Memoir of the Craft*, puts it bluntly: "If you want to be a writer, you must do two things above all others: read a lot and write a lot" (2002, p. 145). Interview after interview, book after book, writers talk about having a place to write every day. For some it's a computer, others a notepad, and still others a notebook. The concept is the same—to have a place just to write ... a lot.

I was speaking to a group of fifth-grade teachers about writing. I was asked to come by this workshop because they were not convinced writing workshop was important. I began by asking how they worked writing into their day. Dead silence. I then asked, How many times do your students write each week? More silence. I continued. How many of you feel your students are prepared for the fifth-grade writing exam? All the hands went up. And so our conversation began. How do you do that? The answer, over and over again, was, We use prompts at least once a month. I then asked, How many of you continue using prompts after the writing exam? Half the hands went up. I cringed at the thought of my next question but asked it anyway: How many of you stop working on writing and focus on grammar or other subject areas after the exam? The other half of the hands went up.

Not only did I need to get these teachers to write daily with their students, but I had to convince them to do so without prompts and to continue writing after the midyear state exam. As our conversation continued and evolved, the same question kept coming up: How do you get students to write? If I don't give them a topic, they just sit there.

Kids are amazingly manipulative. My four-year-old pulls this stunt—I'm ready to take him outside to play, but he needs to put on his shoes. He says he can't find them. I end up finding the shoes buried under toy cars. He then sits down on the floor with one foot up waiting for me to put them on for him so he can play. It occurred to me that I was working a lot harder than he was so that he could go play. It's the same with students and writing: If I'm working harder than they are on their writing, something is terribly wrong.

Don Murray said, "You won't know what you have to say until you write. Writing comes from paying attention." Red Smith writes, "Writing is easy. You sit at the typewriter and open a vein." O. Henry put it best: "Write what makes you happy." Not all writing is happy writing, but O. Henry is saying writing must come from us, not from a book of made-up prompts.

Why Notebooks?

I sometimes wish I was the genius who invented the notebook. Think about it—it's just a bunch of paper (sometimes not even with lines), bound and with a cover. That's it. Paper, binding, cover. GENIUS! Everyone uses them for a thousand different things: grocery lists, math homework, class notes, price quotes, and so on. It's a very mundane item that has become an integral part of our world. If only I owned that patent …

For a writer, the right combination of words, the perfect setting, or the solution to writer's block can come at any time in any place. It's important to have a place to record these bits of life that may serve to inspire further work. That place for us is a writer's notebook.

Writer's notebooks have been written about extensively and called by many different names: scrapbooks, life books, journals, and day books. It's not the name that unifies these but rather the principle behind their use. A writer's notebook creates a place for students (and writers) to save their words—in the form of a memory, a reflection, a list, a rambling of thoughts, a sketch, or even a scrap of print taped on the page. A notebook can become whatever the writer makes it to be. As teachers, we can guide its use, present strategies, and even mandate entries if we wish. If the notebook is to be a useful tool, however, it must be useful to the writer first, and the reader (teacher) second. Because in the long run, the creation of each notebook, each time, is in the hands of the writer.

Teachers often ask me, but what's the point? What am I trying to accomplish with this task? Why is it worthy of so much time every day? Not only are these fair questions, these are questions we should be asking ourselves constantly, every day. With increased curriculum mandates, test pressures, and stagnant school hours, I'm picky and protective of my class time. Writer's notebooks help me maximize the effects of my writing lessons.

A fifth-grade teacher and I were talking about this in the hallway one day. She finally said to me, "I don't need to use notebooks because my kids already write every day."

"Really? How do you accomplish that?" I asked, truly interested.

"Well, they write the answers, in complete sentences, to the questions at the end of each reading story, social studies chapter, and science section," she responded, quite proudly.

"Hmm," was my intelligent response. While inside my head I was shouting, "That doesn't count! That's not what people mean when they say write every day!"

Children's author and educator Lester Laminack visited our school and told the students he was a writ*errrrr*. He writes every day, and I guarantee you *not* by answering questions in a textbook. My students echoed this sentiment in the weeks that passed as we wrote; I would hear whispers of, it's time to be a writ*errrr*. We write every day.

The purpose of a notebook is to provide a place for students to practice writing. It's a place for them to generate text, find ideas, and practice what they know about spelling and grammar. As I have worked with notebooks over the years, I have chosen to use some arbitrary sections that help me organize my thinking within the notebook.

From the beginning of the notebook, I teach my students to practice generating text by using different writing strategies. I rely on some tried-and-true strategies, as well as on the work of writers like Natalie Goldberg, Georgia Heard, Ralph Fletcher, and Anne Lamott.

Building Fluency to Find Significance

Where do people who write acquire all the knowledge they need? The conclusion I reached ... it could only be through reading. —Frank Smith, Joining the Literacy Club

Katie Wood Ray (1996) writes about reading like a writer to improve writing craft. Constance Weaver (2002) has said, for every minute we spend reading, we spend a minute learning about writing and spelling. It's a connection not to be ignored.

One of the biggest pushes in the early primary years is to create reading fluency. Reading fluency is an important skill, not only for reading aloud, but also for reading comprehension. The reading specialist at our school, Cheri Carter, refers to the difference between reading fluency and reading word-for-word as the difference between spreading butter and margarine on a piece of bread. When spreading butter, the bread often tears and the butter is lumped in places on the bread. Margarine goes on smoothly, not tearing the bread, and covers the piece evenly.

I began to realize that writing fluency is equally important for writers. Being able to think and write at the same time—getting words on a page, writing a paragraph, a page, or even a couple of pages in one writer's workshop—is an important skill for students to develop. When children are thinking they are less likely to forget what they want to say. Fluency is the ability to generate text—a lot of it—in a short period of time. This gives students something to work with when it comes to rereading, revising, and even editing. As Lucy Calkins writes: "I write to hold what I find in my life in my hands and to declare it a treasure ... significance cannot be found, it must be grown" (1988, p. 4).

Vicki Vinton says, "It is an illusion that writers live more significant lives than nonwriters; the truth is, writers are just more in the habit of finding the significance that there is in their lives" (Calkins 1988, p. 4).

These are powerful statements offered by Lucy Calkins, who is the kind of teacher I want to be. But statements like these often led me to feel like a failure when it came to keeping notebooks. When I first started keeping my own writer's notebook, it was filled with a lot of ... nothing. Oh, there were words there, a lot of them, but in the first third of the notebook I wrote nothing of significance. Or so it seemed.

I began to worry that I would never be a true writer. So I worked to create the habit of writing. I was writing every day, whether or not I had something "worthy" to say. I studied books about writing and tried the different strategies other authors suggested for practice. I revisited strategies I liked, and dumped the ones I didn't. It got easier and easier to fill the pages of this once-blank notebook. I was creating my own way of writing in the notebook, growing further and further away from the crutch of a diary-like entry or the familiar yearning for a prompt.

And as I filled my notebook, something significant began to happen. I was learning to write fluently—to get text down on paper in order to go back to it. I was rereading, reflecting, and writing some more. I discovered my own ideas and things I wanted to dwell on in my notebook.

When I think about my most reluctant writers, I realize they are the ones who don't write fluently. They have trouble thinking of what to write, or how much to write, or they forget what they wanted to write. From my experiences—and from those of writers everywhere—the most important aspect of a notebook is that it allows students the practice of simply writing ... in whatever form. Writing, writing, writing ...

I now realize what writers have been trying to tell us "nonwriters"—that we shouldn't write for significance, but rather that we should write as a habit. Sometimes we'll write something significant and sometimes we won't. It's the *act* of writing—the practice of generating text and building fluency—that leads writers to significance.

Keeping a notebook isn't something you "get." It's not a science, there is no one right way. Keeping a notebook is a process. It's something that "gets" you—leads you from one thought to another until you, too, experience the writer's joy of discovering something you didn't know you knew.

Chapter 2:

Launching the Notebook

Donald Graves has an uncanny ability to keep focused on what is important about teaching writing. Despite the media's continual reminders that students today do not punctuate well, use proper grammar, or spell correctly, Graves (2002) sees the writing "crisis" as even more devastating than problems students have with surface features: people do not see themselves as writers because they believe they have nothing valuable or of interest to others to say. I keep this thought in mind as I start each school year, knowing my foremost task with my writing workshop is to help my students believe in themselves as writers—in what they have to say, from the stories they have to tell to their opinions on school and world issues.

Desks pushed aside, my fourth-grade students and I create a circle on the carpet in the middle of the classroom. We begin the year with storytelling. Oral storytelling allows children to tell about themselves and their experiences, and helps me take note of oral language skills while learning about each child. Throughout the first week of school, we spend a lot of time telling stories.

To get storytelling off to a good start, I read aloud a lot of picture books. One book I use is *Enemy Pie* by Derek Munson (2000). It's about a little boy looking forward to a summer playing with his best friend ... until Jeremy Ross moves into the neighborhood and becomes archenemy number one. Luckily, Dad has a plan to make enemy pie, if only the little boy can be nice to Jeremy for one whole day. As it turns out, he and Jeremy become friends and Dad's enemy pie is delicious!

"Has that ever happened to you?" I begin after reading the book. "Has one of your parents ever tricked you into doing something?" Most heads nod; a few children stare blankly back. This is one of the first days of school, and my students are still not sure how much to participate.

I continue. "Sometimes I trick my son, Mikey. The other day he didn't want to eat his green beans. All he wanted was dessert. He cried, he whined, he even threw a fit when I said, 'It's the green beans or no dessert.' Can you believe it?" I pause, partly for effect and partly to look around and make sure everyone is listening. "Finally, I whispered, 'I have a secret.' Even above his tantrum he heard me.

"'WHAT?' he asked.

"I looked around, pretending to make sure no one was listening. Then I told him, 'Green beans give you superpowers, like Batman.'" My students start giggling. I continue with my story. "'If you eat your green beans, it will help your muscles grow tonight.'

"Mikey looked at me and asked, 'What about dessert? Does dessert give me superpowers?'

"'Nope,' I told him, 'green beans do.' And wouldn't you know it, Mikey ate every one of his green beans." The kids laugh that Mikey fell for my little trick.

I ask my students again, "Who can tell us about a time when your parents tricked you? Or a sibling?" I always add someone else to the list, as some children feel more comfortable telling stories about things that happen to their siblings or friends. Eventually, as they feel more comfortable in the classroom, their stories turn to themselves.

I take notes in my notebook—things I want to remember—as each child speaks. Somewhere along the way, someone is bound to ask, What are you writing? I tell them I'm writing about them, noting connections I have to their stories. Like when Courtney told us about basketball camp, I say, I remembered when I played basketball in middle school. That was a long time ago, and I haven't thought about it in a while. It may be something I'll want to write about later.

Generally, students will respond with an "Oh," as if to say, "That's weird and let's move on." So we do. But I continue to take notes, make connections, and write ideas in my notebook. Finally, on Friday of the first week, Nate asks me, "Are you going to write in that every day?"

"Yes," I reply.

"What are you writing about today?" he continues.

And so I read to him about the connection I had made as Ashley talked about getting stuck in a traffic jam because of construction. She went on to talk about what her family did to entertain themselves, and I remembered a time I was stuck in traffic due to construction. Cars were at a dead stop because the two left lanes were closed, leaving only one lane open. The traffic snaked up a hill and beyond that, for all I knew. Suddenly, I heard a siren. I looked in my rearview mirror and saw an ambulance coming. There was nowhere to go to get out of the way. I wondered what the ambulance would do.

"What happened?" asks Nate.

"I haven't finished yet," I reply, "but I will later tonight."

A sea of hands begins to wave, as other students, talking all at once, remember stories of traffic trauma. I settle the children down and tell them I have a solution. We can't all talk at once, and we don't have time to hear everyone's story, but I do have a way for them to save their stories so they won't forget. Out come my stacks of notebooks. "Each one of you is getting a notebook today. This notebook is for your stories, ideas, and thinking. It's a writer's notebook, much like my own." As I hand each child a notebook, I don't get a lot of moans and groans because just a minute ago they all had a story to tell. That's the secret to getting kids into notebooks. Have them tell stories to each other, keep notes and ideas in your own notebook, share them with your kids, and wait for the right moment, when it seems that everyone has a story to tell.

Inside Notebooks

The physical form of the notebook can reflect the teacher's preference and is generally inconsequential to the concept. Many people—writers and students alike—have preferences. I prefer that students use composition notebooks because the pages are sewn into the notebook so that none can be ripped out. A close friend of mine, who teaches high school, prefers a binder for her students' writer's notebooks. She likes kids to be able to add pages when going back to work on a certain entry or to put handouts and class notes near the entries where they'll have the greatest impact. Still other excellent writing teachers prefer that their students write on notebook paper and store everything in a folder.

The type of notebook a teacher chooses needs to reflect his or her teaching and organization style. Even though the notebooks will ultimately be in the hands of the writer, the teacher needs to make it work with curriculum, classroom space, and time.

When planning for notebooks, there are several things for teachers to consider. I use a series of questions and responses (Figure 2–1) to help me think through the feasibility of the notebook my class will use. (There is a blank chart with the same questions in the appendix for your own considerations.)

Figure 2–1 *Considerations for Notebooks*

Is it easily portable to take home and bring back to school?	I find that it's important for students to take the notebook with them. I like a lightweight and easy-to-carry notebook.
Does it provide a standard-sized page?	I didn't always think this was important until students argued that some kids don't really write as much because their pages are smaller or thinner. To keep the peace, I require a standard-sized notebook.
Is it easily replaceable when it becomes filled?	Expect notebooks to be filled. Even if it's a binder, you will want it replaced. There's something wonderful about a brand-new notebook. Make sure they're easily accessible.
Is it a size that will be easy for you to collect and read?	You will need to read these and even assess them. Keep in mind how you will collect and store them if necessary.
Do you have a plan for where students will put their class notes and/or handouts?	Some teachers like to put notes and handouts near certain existing entries. I have kids keep notes in the back of their notebook for easy reference. Handouts are cut down and glued into the notebook.
Will students be able to personalize the notebook?	It may not seem important, but it is. Students should have the ability to make this notebook their own—inside and out. Composition notebooks now have different-style covers and are easily covered with stickers and/or construction paper.
Is it important to take pages in and out of the notebook? Does your notebook support this?	If this is important to you, you may want to use a binder or folder. I don't want pages coming in or out, so I stick with a bound notebook.
Is the notebook easy for all students to manage?	All students are expected to keep a notebook. If there are special needs to consider, be sure to do so. One year I needed to arrange for a student to keep his notebook on a computer.

I'm careful to keep the organization of the notebooks flexible, without a lot of superficial or arbitrary sections. This was difficult for me at first because it seemed it would be easier to use a sectioned, three-subject notebook with different parts for different assignments. I have gone so far as to use sticky tabs and paper clips to mark off pages. But I have found over the years that the notebook rarely fills up if you do this. Some sections have paper left over, and kids are using one notebook for entries, another for lists, another for favorite words, and so on. It gets very confusing.

In addition, it is important for students to fill a notebook—really fill it. As overwhelming as the panic of what to write about can be when flipping through the blank pages of a new notebook, the sense of achievement is equally strong when students flip through a notebook that is filled with their words on every page from beginning to end. Finishing a writer's notebook, truly finishing it, is as important to a writer as finishing a book is to a reader.

I am a person who likes routine—many writers are. I like having a routine with the notebooks, so that students can readily transfer learning from the notebooks to their drafts in progress. With this in mind, I ask the students to have two starting points. Students write from the front of the notebook toward the back with their daily, self-selected topics. Here students date each page and title entries when appropriate. Students can also try the different strategies presented in class—interwoven with their own ways of keeping a notebook. Some students glue a table of contents in the inside cover, listing the strategies, their dates and the page numbers where they can be found. Others simply keep a list of the strategies we study on the inside cover. Still others just keep a hodgepodge in the notebook, with no indications of where things are located.

The second starting point is from the back of the notebook, working toward the front. Here we keep notes from lessons, such as revision strategies, editing strategies, and grammar notes. Examples of good writing from other texts can be found in both sections, depending on the purpose—if we're looking at craft it may go in the mix with our regular entries; if it is a piece that emphasizes a strategy we're focusing on, such as paragraph structure, it would go in the back. When working from the back of the notebook on editing and revision strategies:

1. Students take notes on the mini-lesson;
2. Students try the revision or editing strategy in their notebooks with a common text;
3. Students go back to their writing to use the strategy; and
4. Students refer to their notebooks as a resource when trying the new strategy.

This gives me not only a structure for teaching strategies and using the notebook, but also a reference when conferring with students. If they say they're having trouble with a lead, I can ask, Did you review our notes on grabber leads? Did you review the "Try Ten" strategy? Did you use it for this piece? Or, if a student is struggling with endings and I haven't focused my mini-lessons on that yet, I can still refer to what I know is in the notebook: Let's review the "Try Ten" strategy we used for leads. Do you think you can use this strategy to help with your ending?

No matter where we are in the writing process, our notebooks are not far away. And the front and back starting points make use of every available page by the time the notebook is filled.

Other than introducing these two methods, I leave the organization up to the kids. Sometimes, students will use Post-it notes to make tabs for lists, poetry, special stories, and so on. Other times they'll use paper clips to save pages for certain ideas or strategies. Some students do not use any other form of organization beyond my front/back method. When it comes to notebooks, less is more, so keep it simple and focus on what's important—students are writing. Students in my fourth-grade classroom will usually fill two notebooks a year.

Figure 2–2 What's In? What's Out?	
In the Notebook	Out of the Notebook
Daily Entries—strategies for launching the notebook	Drafts The whole piece is written out on yellow legal-pad paper.
Finding Patterns—rereading and marking patterns in writing	Revisions Revisions the author wants to use are added or deleted from the piece.
Collecting Around a Topic—strategies for thinking about a topic	
Revision Strategies—trying different things for a draft	Editing Editing the actual piece before writing the final copy is done right on the draft.
Editing, Grammar Notes—class notes on grammar and editing skills	Final Copy Final copies of writing pieces are done on white paper or another published format.

One question teachers ask is, "How will students know where to find things in their notebooks?" A binder or a three-section notebook would indeed make it easier to find things. However, as students keep notebooks and work with them on a regular basis, they become familiar with them. Much like rereading your favorite novel until you know about where a certain event is in the text, students have a general knowledge of where things are. Students reread, which every good writer should do, and find what they need as they need it. It hasn't been a big deal. Kids who want things more organized can use paper clips, sticky notes, or a table of contents and index techniques. But overall our notebooks are a reflection of our lives—there is enough organization to keep them functional and enough flexibility to keep them interesting.

Strategies for Beginning Notebook Writing

I take a lot of time to teach students different strategies for finding things to write about in the notebook. These strategies help writers look at their lives and their world in a way that seeks out stories, poems, and ideas. Unlike a prompt, a strategy can be used again and again in different contexts with different results.

I usually introduce three or four strategies before letting the kids fly solo. This way, when I do have a quick mini-lesson and say, "Go write," students will have an idea of what they can do. Students must be convinced they have something to write about, so I start with what I refer to as my no-fail strategies. Everyone and anyone can write with these strategies, which include History of a Name, Writing from a List, and Questions.

History of a Name

Gathering the children on the carpet once again, I remind them of a story we read earlier, *Chrysanthemum* by Kevin Henkes (1996). "Why do you think the author chose to write about a child's name?" I ask.

Hands go up and Sarah responds first. "Well, it's like you said, to remind us that names are special and we shouldn't tease each other."

"That may be one reason, can you think of another?" I prod.

Students look at each other and then Cameron raises his hand, "Maybe because he thinks names are special. Chrysanthemum's parents loved her name and loved her."

"I think you're right, Cameron. Names are special. I know I took a lot of time thinking about my son's name. I bet your parents did the same for you."

"I know how I got my name," Chi Chi pipes in, "It's from Nigeria where my dad grew up. Chineyre—but I go by Chi Chi."

I look around, "Today in your notebook, I'd like you to try writing about your name. Maybe you can tell us where your name comes from, like Chi Chi did. Maybe your name has a special meaning. Think about it and go write."

As the students begin, I walk around to confer with those who are having trouble starting, like Rex.

"Rex, how's it going?" I ask.

"I don't know."

"What don't you know?" I try to get kids to be specific, even on the second day of actually writing.

"I don't know what to do."

This is a typical first conference. Students who have not had the expectation to write from their own experiences sometimes have trouble getting started, even with a strategy like writing about your name. I believe they are afraid of being wrong. No one likes to redo work, so sometimes it's easier to just not do it.

"Rex. That's an interesting name."

"It's not my real name. My real name is Antonio."

"Ooh, like the actor Antonio Banderas. He's one of my favorites."

"Huh? My real mom named me Antonio but my mom now calls me Rex."

Now that Rex is ready to talk I stop him. "Rex, stop right there. It sounds like you are on the verge of telling me about your name."

"I guess I am."

"Go ahead and start writing."

After a few more quick conferences to make sure everyone is on task, I ask students to stop writing for just a moment. I ask for volunteers to share what they have started. This helps clarify the assignment for those who are still confused and confirms for others that they're on the right track (Figure 2–3). Ashley begins.

> *Everyone thinks my name is a pretty name. I don't think it's everything I am. I like sports, but I don't see sports in my name. What I do like about my name is that it has six letters. The rainbow has six colors. So I can put the colors in my name. I love the rainbow that's why I like at least some of my name. I wonder why my parents named me Ashley?*

Figure 2–3 *Launching Strategy: History of a Name*

How: Students put their name or a family name at the top of a notebook and write about it—how they got their name, what they like about their name, what they don't like about their name or nickname.

Why? The naming of something or someone is significant for writers. Understanding the history of a name leads to deeper understanding of that topic.

Extensions: Read aloud *Frindle* by Andrew Clements; ponder names of characters in read-aloud books; consider the names of inventions or new products.

Using this strategy, kids often start looking at how they named their pets, names they wished they had, and even how their last names came to be. The naming of someone or something is significant, and writers are choosy about characters' names. With a new interest in names, many students choose to work with this strategy for another day or two.

Writing from a List

Another important strategy is Writing from a List. This is something kids have experience with from previous years. Many times students have kept a list of writing prompts, ideas, words, and questions. But I have found that students will not initiate starting these lists—they are usually the result of teacher prompts.

I start this lesson by, once again, gathering the kids on the floor in front of me. They are already picking up the routine of sitting on the floor with their notebooks and pens. With my notebook and pen in hand, I begin the mini-lesson on lists.

"Today we're going to try another strategy. It's called writing from a list."

"We did that last year," pipes up Matthew.

"Great, because I use this strategy whenever I get stuck. I've found it very helpful, so if you've used it before, you'll be good at using it again." I don't find it annoying when kids chime in that they've done something before in another class. As a writer grows and changes, so do their lists and approaches to writing. Their previous experience with the strategy builds their confidence and affirms the activity for others. I continue, "Please date your notebook and write 'Best Life Events' on the top." I wait a moment as students write this down; I want everyone to keep together initially, as they learn this strategy. "Now, for this list I want you to try to jot down the ten best things that have ever happened to you. If nothing fabulous has ever happened, then choose ten really good things. Begin."

I begin a list in my notebook. I look up from time to time to make sure students are writing and/or thinking. Amazingly enough, this is a difficult list for many children to make. After a couple of minutes, I stop and ask for volunteers to share one thing on their lists. This is important to do, because students may say something that others will connect with. It helps keep students generating ideas without getting stuck. We go back to write for another two minutes or so. Students do not always finish the list in the time permitted. That's okay. They can go back and add to it at home or during a workshop time in which they're stuck for something to write about.

After each child has an opportunity to share an event on his or her list, I direct the students to put a star near each event they could write more about. Then we move on to the next list: Seven Worst Events. This list fills up more quickly for students. I follow the same procedure I used with the good events.

As students take ownership of this strategy, the topics for lists begin to get more interesting and more personal. Students will list their friends, their favorite video games, or things they want for their birthday.

Here is an example from Colleen's notebook:

8/18 Best List	Worst List
1. My mom	1. Getting stitches*
2. All of my pets*	2. Chelsea dying*
3. My old home	3. Sliced with weapon of death*
4. My dad	4. Snake inside*
5. My new home	5. Getting stitches, again*
6. Catie	6. Leaving St. Louis*
7. Kelly being born*	7. Stung by a jellyfish*
8. My fish	
9. Chelsea*	
10. Living in St. Louis*	

"Now look at the things you put a star near. When you write from a list, it means to take an event or item from your list, write it on a new page, then write the story behind it. So for today, I want you to try this. Choose something from either list and write an entry about it. When you finish, you can repeat the strategy or write about something else that is on your mind."

It's important that students finish trying the strategy even if they have something else to write about. When I give a mini-lesson, I want students to try it out in their notebooks, so they have experience with the skill and a personal example to which to refer (Figure 2–4).

Figure 2–4 *Launching Strategy: Writing from a List*

How: Students make a quick list based on a self-selected topic. List topics might include things they are experts on, best events in their lives, worst events, favorite words. They star or highlight things on their list they could write more about. Students then write an entry on those ideas.

Why? This is an easy, reasonable task even for students who struggle as writers. It is a strategy that can be used again and again for generating idea topics.

Extensions: Lists can be used when students are drafting any written piece, to dive deeper into the topic, to collect words, quotes, and trivia that can be used later in the piece, and even to explore nonfiction possibilities.

As students maintain this strategy, lists range from the movies they have seen to their favorite words. Sometimes I'll find a list of video games and a rating system next to it. Students use these lists to keep track of hobbies or ideas they don't want to lose but have no other means of organizing. The key part of this strategy, though, is that students learn to use these lists to jump-start other entries.

Courtney has some interesting lists in her notebook that stray from the best and worst lists.

Scary Stories
- falling down the stairs
- skipping a step on the stairs
- when my grandpa died
- when there is a storm
- when my brother's frogs get out of their cage
- when I go to my grandma's house and when I go to bed, I feel like I'm going to get kidnapped because there are no men there
- dreams
- beaches
- when a softball hits your head

Sarah uses one item from her list, her first birthday party, to begin her entry:

My First Birthday Party
I had my first birthday party when I turned six. My mom served us sugar cookies that we got to frost ourselves. My friend, Sarah, put frosting all over her face and ran around our house screaming, "I'm a witch!" It was so funny! Then she finally went to the bathroom to look. All she said was, "Cool." It was the best party I ever had!

At first, students will do a lot of shallow writing, like Sarah's entry above. It used to frustrate me. I wanted deep thinking, reflective writing, and creativity immediately. I have come to realize that this is not how learning to write well works. Students are going to write shallow, simple entries. They're going to do what they think you want. Keep plugging away and keep showing examples of high-quality writing. When a student writes a meaningful entry, copy it, with their permission, and share it.

Here is Colleen's entry about Chelsea dying, from her worst list:

8/18 Chelsea's Heart

Three days after my birthday, my dad came home extremely upset. My mom was in the kitchen and Catie and I were in the basement.

My dad had taken my dog, Chelsea, to the vet's earlier that day. Chelsea had heart problems earlier in her life. But that day her heart had broken down.

Catie and I burst out in tears!! We cried our eyes out!! We never got to say good-bye to her. Even though she is in heaven, I'll still love her until I die.

In my heart, I left a spot open for her. Not deep down, but way up in the front.

Questions

Has this ever happened to you? It's mid-afternoon and I'm in the middle of a social studies lesson. Students are spread out around the room with desk maps and markers everywhere, as we work to track the Lewis and Clark expedition. Suddenly an arm starts waving frantically. "Ms. Buckner! Ms. Buckner!"

"Yes?" I reply as I hurry over, thinking this group made a discovery of some sort to share with the class.

"We were just wondering when we could choose our own seats. Our group wants to sit together all the time."

My first thought is, you have got to be kidding me. We're in the middle of a social studies lesson on the Lewis and Clark expedition, and they are thinking about what it would be like to sit together all of the time? I answer quickly, "I'm glad your group is working well together. For now, stay focused on the expedition at hand."

Whether or not one is a great teacher, we cannot control what kids think about at any given time. They wonder about a lot of things, and sometimes it is frustrating. I don't particularly want children wondering why we can't have more recess when we need to discuss the events leading to the Revolutionary War. But the fact is, kids think all the time, and it's not always about school.

Capturing their questions, their general "wonders," in their writer's notebooks allows students to reflect and think more deeply. When I introduce this notebook strategy, students usually want to make a list of questions—brief and to the point. The goal of this mini-lesson is to teach students to take one question or one thing they wonder about and try to think through it—to write what might possibly be the answer or what thinking led them to this question in the first place (Figure 2–5).

Debbie Miller writes about wonder boxes in her book *Reading with Meaning* (2002). These boxes are 3-by-5-inch file boxes containing brightly colored cards on which her first graders record their questions and wonderings. She believes the secret of wisdom is to be curious:

> *Children everywhere know that the secret of wisdom is to be curious about the world, to open up their senses and see, hear, taste, touch and smell life's treasures. … My job is to continue to nurture their wonder and work to awaken my own. (p. 135)*

In the example below, Erin explores the "wonder" of whether or not Adam and Eve had belly buttons. Her mother was pregnant at the time, and Erin had taken a big-sister class that explained how and why we have belly buttons.

Erin:

Have you ever wondered if Adam and Eve had belly buttons? I mean, of course, I learned in Sunday School that they were the first two people on Earth. God made them as adults. They were not born out of someone's stomach. If they were, then I am sure they would have belly buttons. They could because when they had a child the child would have a belly button, and they might think that their child was odd and they would possibly kill it. Well, maybe no one back then, in Bible times, had belly buttons.

In the next example, Mac wonders about communicating with his cat. This entry came after a night when his parents were discussing the endless barking of a dog in the neighborhood.

●◆ Mac:

Why do cats meow? Do cats talk or is it an involuntary spasm? Or is it voluntary? I think they're trying to tell us something. My cat starts meowing, and I feed him. He shuts up. But sometimes he keeps meowing. I give him everything and he still won't stop. Meow meow meow!

Figure 2–5   *Launching Strategy: Questioning*

How: Students think of the questions or situations they have always wondered about and record their thinking in the entry. Not all questions have easy answers, so students try to think through them. For questions that have specific answers, students can use their notebook to collect some research on the question at hand.

Why? Our minds wander. As a child I was always told to stay focused. But wandering minds think interesting things. The questioning strategy encourages students to think out of the box, to probe deeper into "facts" they take for granted, and to stretch their thinking beyond daily events.

Extensions: Students can research answers to some questions, or use this technique to generate probing interview questions. This kind of questioning and thinking leads to a deeper understanding of more sophisticated topics, such as history or current events; so it's a good strategy to integrate into other curriculum areas.

Building Writing Fluency and Sustaining Interest

Storytelling, writing about a name, writing from a list, and thinking through questions are strategies I use to launch the notebook. Once it is launched, I then begin introducing strategies to help maintain the notebook. These are strategies I've noticed children using more regularly. They are strategies that tend to help students generate text and to build up their writing fluency. They include Daily Pages, Writing off Literature, Observations, Writing from a Word, Rereading and Highlighting, and Lifting a Line.

Daily Pages

To live a creative life, we must lose our fear of being wrong. —Joseph Chilton Pearce

The fear of being wrong is the most difficult thing for students to get over. By fourth grade, or even earlier, students have determined that if they do the task correctly the first time they won't have to do it over. "Doing it right," to them, means perfect spelling, being neat, and knowing what to say so the teacher likes it. This is the wrong attitude for a notebook, and will result in perfectly mundane entries that mean little to students or anyone else.

Daily Pages is an idea I adopted from Julia Cameron's *The Artist's Way* (1992). For this mini-lesson, students are required to write a minimum of one page every day before writing workshop. A whole page—no skipping lines, no starting three or four lines from the top, and no writing so big that you only fit three words on a line. A whole, normal-size page, which holds approximately one hundred words. (No, I don't count, but it impresses the kids.) Generally, they have time during morning arrival to do this. Or students might do it at home before coming to school.

The point of this exercise for students is to take their trash out, to clear their minds. They might write about the routine soccer practice or the play-by-play of Monday night football, or about being bored at school or having no time for breakfast. If a student has nothing to write about in the morning, chances are he or she won't have anything to write about in a couple of hours either. So it's okay to spend the morning writing about nothing on the daily page, as long as you are ready to write something during writing workshop (Figure 2–6).

Figure 2–6   *Fluency Strategy: Daily Pages*

How: Provide students with ten to fifteen minutes at the beginning of each day simply to write whatever comes to mind. This writing should be predictable and dependable so that it becomes part of their writing habit.

Why? In order to get to our more creative and thoughtful selves, we need to clear out the cobwebs that life leaves in our heads and that cloud our thinking. The everyday bus incidents, sibling arguments, homework anxiety, and soccer practice have to be thought through before students are able to think more deeply and write more fluently.

Extensions: Students can continue this practice at home on the weekends or over holiday breaks. Students might also do daily pages at the end of the day to reflect on the school day in addition to the morning pages.

Don't expect too much from these pages at first. This is where students will hide the most. They'll bore themselves silly writing about things of little importance to them.

⬤◆ **8/22 My Weekend**
*On Saturday we went to lots of places. First my little sister had
to got to a birthday party at American Adventure from 2:00–8:00.
After they left, we went to the hardware store to get some
stuff to hang our hammock chair. We also had to get some grill
starting gas.*

Eventually, they will anticipate and plan for these pages. Getting through the mundane will be easier and less of a burden. Creativity will begin to leak out and then ... a page will not be nearly enough to contain it.

Writing off Literature

Writers read a lot. In order to get students writing, I also need to get them reading. All too often, teachers think of reading aloud as a primary-age activity. Or, in the upper grades, reading aloud has to involve a novel with questions for each chapter to make sure kids are listening.

We know from the work of Harvey and Goudvis (2000) that good readers are thinking while they read. And if they're thinking, they have something to write about. So it's important to give students a chance to listen to stories, poems, or articles and to write about their thinking. Stories inspire stories.

I share a lot of picture books and poetry in the beginning of the year. They're short and don't eat away at the writing workshop. When writing off literature, I often use text students have not heard before. I want to get fresh reactions. I will read the text twice before they write. This is how it goes:

Gathered around on the floor, notebooks and pencils in hand, we begin the day's mini-lesson. "We read a lot of stories and poems in school. Does anyone sometimes think that you might have a story to write, like the one you just heard?" I ask.

Hands go up and heads nod. I continue, "It happens to me too. Today I'm going to read a poem by Alice Schertle called, 'Keepers' from her poetry anthology *Keepers* (1996). I'll read it twice. The first time, I want you just to listen to the poem. Enjoy it as a reader. The second time I read it, I want you to also listen, but if you have an idea, a connection, or something you want to write, you can go ahead and do that. When I'm finished reading the poem the second time, we're not going to talk about it at all. We're just going to write."

Heads nod and I begin. I read the poem once and no one writes. Students listen and think. The second time I read the poem, some students listen to it all the way through, while others begin to write in their notebooks (Figure 2–7).

Here is Ryan's entry:

●← Reflection on "Keepers" by Alice Schertle

I liked this poem because it had to do with fishing. I also really like the title "Keeper." I like the sound of it. I could say it all day. I liked that the little boy that went fishing told the story, not the author. This is my favorite part, "His round eye had a startled look. He gulped the painful air." These two sentences tell you, you do not want to be a fish. It is also very descriptive, the words from these two sentences I like are: startled, gulped, and painful. Another part I liked, "and wished I could slip him over board but I didn't dare." I wonder if he thought his dad would get mad if he slipped the fish overboard.

Figure 2–7   Fluency Strategy: Writing off Literature

How: Begin by telling students that after you read you want them to write. Share some favorite picture books, short stories, poems, or novels with your class that leave the reader thinking even after the text is finished. Then, as you finish reading aloud, without a sound or another instruction, students begin to write. Sometimes teachers may want to focus the writing with a prompt, and I caution you before doing that—often students think far beyond what is expected of a ready-made writing response.

Why? Good literature causes people to think, relate, and dwell in the story. As writers, we must also be readers, and allow ourselves to be affected by what we read. If students are to write about their experiences in a way that will engage an audience, they must allow their own reading to engage them.

Extensions: Students may want to write a memory that was spurred by the story. You can use wonderful student writing (with student permission) to do the same. Read editorials aloud and ask students to respond. Read newspaper articles that spur your own thinking and allow students to write.

Observations

Once again, I gather my students around me for a mini-lesson. I have several books we have read before—*Twilight Comes Twice* by Ralph Fletcher (1997), *The Great Frog Race* by Kristine O'Connell George (1997), and Byrd Baylor's *I'm in Charge of Celebrations* (1995). My students have their notebooks in front of them, and most have already turned to a clean page and written the date. Before any of them ask if we're going to read these books again, I begin.

"Boys and girls, we have read these three books several times. Today I'd like us to predict what kind of notebook entries might have led to these books."

No hands go up, and finally Sarah says what they are all thinking, "I'm not sure I understand, Ms. Buckner."

"How do you think the seed idea for these books looked in the author's notebook? Do you think they stemmed from a question? a list? a memory?"

"Not a memory for any of them," replies Christopher. "These are all like poetry books."

"To me they are things the author sees," Kelsey quietly adds.

"You may be right, Kelsey," I say. All of these books help the reader observe the world in a way they may not have thought to before. When I talk to authors or read interviews, I have noticed a piece of advice that seems to keep coming up."

"I know, I know ... read," Nate says in that irritated, bored way fourth graders have.

"Yes, but there is something else: Pay attention to the world around you. Writers notice what regular people don't. Writers use their five senses to truly observe what is going on around them. They try to paint images with words— not just any words, the right words. Being aware of one's surroundings and being able to write about them actually take practice—a lot of practice."

Sarah pipes in, "So let me guess ... we're going to practice!"

"Yes, today we're going to work on recording observations."

Children's recorded observations, like their beginning lists, may at first be bland and ordinary. Since I often take several days to teach children how to be good observers, I don't panic. During the second mini-lesson with observations, I put emphasis on using sensory language, similes, and even metaphors as students begin. We also take time to investigate narrative observations (Figure 2–8).

Kelsey's Observations in a List

The candles flicker in the night like they're excited.
Leaves fall off the trees crisp and dead.
Trees dance as the wind blows.
Ice moves in the refrigerator like rocks falling off the mountain.
Lights flicker off the Christmas tree like lights off the ocean.

Michael's Pencil Sharpener Observation

The Pencil Sharpener Next Door
Well, I keep hearing this noise in Mrs. Zieg's room. Dave asked,
"What is that?" Mrs. Buckner said, "the pencil sharpener." I said,
"It's pretty loud." It keeps going and going. Someone must really
need to sharpen their pencil. In our room, no one sharpens their
pencil that much. It keeps going every 5 seconds. It just stopped.
It's still going a little though. Someone's probably sharpening
their pencil to the eraser, and they're doing a good job.

Figure 2–8 *Fluency Strategy: Observations*

How: Make students more aware of their surroundings by reminding them that writers use their senses all the time. Students might start by making a list of things they observe or drawing quick sketches with captions.

Why? Writers need to create moods, settings, and pictures in the readers' minds. Being aware of the world around them, how to describe it, and just thinking about the possibilities the observations pose bring greater depth to student writing, help students develop their pieces more substantially, and give them practice at drawing pictures with words.

Extensions: Observe one item—the same item—over time. Using magazine pictures, paintings, or other visuals, have students practice using observations to create the same image in a reader's mind. Then, ask them to apply this strategy to their own writing by taking a part of their story and drawing a picture. Do the words match the picture?

Writing from A Word

My friend Judy Eggemeier and I taught next to each other for several years. We both taught language arts to sixth graders at the local middle school. Our rooms were divided by a movable wall. I could hear her giving a mini-lesson as I was giving mine and would find myself repeating some of her words of wisdom. (It was a thin wall.)

Judy took a writing class at Miami University of Ohio with Tom Romano. Every Wednesday night she'd go to class and every Thursday we'd open our wall to hear what happened in her class the night before. Sixty sixth graders and two teachers sat in a circle, waiting for the college-level lesson about writing.

It was in this circle that Judy showed us how to write from a word. I have had so much success with this personally that sharing it with my students years later, in an elementary school hundreds of miles from Judy, now seems natural.

Figure 2–9   *Fluency Strategy: Writing from a Word*

How: Choose a noun, any noun, and put it at the top of the page. Ask the students to write for twenty minutes or so. If your class is still building their writing stamina, make it fifteen, but no less. During this timed writing, students are to think about the word then begin writing. The goal is to write for the entire period, even if the topic meanders away from the original word.

Why? When writers have writer's block, they often need help getting through that stage. This strategy is easy to use and easy to remember how to do. Plus, it doesn't matter if you stay on topic—it is totally stream-of-consciousness writing. Students are amazed, not only at the amount of writing they do with this strategy but also at the topics that pop up in their writing.

Extensions: This strategy can be extended to any kind of word: verbs, adverbs, adjectives, etc.

Ask the children to choose a noun, any noun, and just a noun. Then, for the next twenty minutes or so, write. Warn students that it may be hard at first and seemingly meaningless, but that it is very important to write the whole time. Also, ask students not to worry about crossing things out or editing, just to let the power of the word lead them. Finally, let them know that it is okay to move off the topic, that this often happens to writers as the mind begins to wander—follow that mind (Figure 2–9)!

☛ Cameron Writing on a Word: COWS

My favorite animals are cows. I don't know why, but they are. Cows come in lots of different colors too. (Especially at the cow parade in downtown Atlanta.) If I talked about how much I like cows for as long as I could, it probably wouldn't be very long. That doesn't mean I don't like them a lot though.

I have a cow collection too. So far, I have 9 things in my cow collection. A cow superball, a cow pillow, a cow lollipop that I got one or two years ago, 4 cow animals, a cow pen, and a cow stamp. I wonder what I'll get for my collection next! Anyway, I like cows.

Rereading and Highlighting

Rereading the notebook is an important strategy for writers. When writers reread, they often notice incomplete entries that need finishing. Sometimes they'll find an entry they want to write more about or think about in a different way. As students grow and change, the way they look at things will change, too. So rereading a notebook for inspiration should not be overlooked. I find it helpful to be specific the first time I ask students to reread as a strategy to maintain their writer's notebooks.

I often begin new mini-lessons by saying, "I've been thinking." A few groans usually fill the air, as students anticipate work from my thinking. "Writers often reread their notebooks to find ideas to write about. When you write every day, you may put something in an entry that doesn't seem significant but that later becomes something you want to dwell on a bit more."

"Like when I found a line of poetry in my observations?" asks Steven, always eager to please.

"Sort of. When we wrote one-line observations, we were working like poets, so when you reread you did find lines of poetry waiting to be explored." I begin handing out highlighters to each student. Excited murmurs about this new tool float through the air. "I want you to reread your notebook today. Use your highlighter to mark any line you think is interesting or that you could write more from. If questions or other reflections pop into your head, write them in the margins of the entry with a pencil or pen."

"Why are we doing this?" asks Matthew.

"Because seed ideas, just like poems, tend to hide." And so they go off to reread and highlight.

My students reread their notebooks for a lot of different reasons—to find ideas for writing, to find patterns, and for self-evaluations. Rereading allows children to revisit their thinking. As adults we know we think about many situations more than once—we rehearse arguments, relive celebrations, and reconsider decisions. We assume children do this too, but they don't. For them, it's as if once the story is written down, it is over. You can't add on weeks later or change your mind. I'm not sure why students think this way, but after years of teaching, I still have to teach rereading and revisiting entries as a strategy.

Once students reread their notebooks, many will begin writing immediately. They find entries they didn't finish or ones they want to add on to.

They find entries about being excited about a birthday party and want to go back to write what actually happened. Rereading keeps the notebook alive and well (Figure 2–10).

> **Figure 2–10** *Fluency Strategy: Rereading and Highlighting*
>
> **How:** Students find a quiet place and reread their notebook from beginning to end. They read each page and every word. Students highlight interesting lines or ideas that they want to dwell on in another entry. Students also may choose to write themselves notes or questions in the margins of entries to revisit later.
>
> **Why?** Writers need to get in the habit of rereading their work—word for word. Students are able to revisit entries they had wanted to write more about but had forgotten. Students often leave questions in margins that echo the questions I'll ask in conferences. In addition, they often find some old ideas they want to think about in a new way.
>
> **Extensions:** This is a good strategy to use on drafts as well. It helps writers find parts of their work that need to be developed further or that can be written from a different angle. This strategy helps keep writing fresh.

Lifting a Line

The next day, I'll pose another strategy. "Remember yesterday I asked you to reread and highlight lines from your writing?" I ask. Heads nod as kids begin flipping through their notebooks, anticipating they'll need one of those lines. "Go ahead and find one that you think you could write more about."

I wait until most students have stopped flipping and seem to have something to work with. "Now, I want you to lift that line. I'm going to show you how. Who is willing to share theirs?"

Christopher raises his hand and begins reading, "We walk onto the field bold and confident."

"Wow. That is a great line. Why did you highlight it?"

"Well, I was surprised that I wrote it. I found it in an entry about a soccer game. I like the way it sounds."

"Okay. Here is what you'll do. Christopher is going to rewrite his line on the top of a clean page in his notebook." I demonstrate this on the easel. This instruction seems easy enough, but I always try to teach the obvious and for this lesson that means writing the line on the top of a clean sheet of chart paper.

"Today, Christopher is going to use this as his lead sentence for a new entry. He'll start with 'We walked onto the field bold and confident,' and continue the entry from there" (Figure 2–11).

We walked onto the field bold and confident staring down the other team. We were prepared to win. This was a playoff game. This was the last game before the championship. Our coach said, to be champions we must think like champions. That day, that game, we were champions from the moment we stepped on the field. The whistle blew and we showed why we were destined to win.

Figure 2–11   *Fluency Strategy: Lifting a Line*

How: After rereading and highlighting, students look at the sentences they highlighted throughout their notebooks. Choosing one that is interesting or easy to write about, the writer recopies the highlighted sentence onto the next clean page. (This may not be juxtaposed to the page it was highlighted on and that's okay.) The "lifted" sentence is now the first line of a new entry.

Why? This gives the writer a fresh starting place with an idea that may have been lost in another entry. It also helps writers to develop their ideas as their fluency skills improve.

Extensions: Students can find sentences they wish they had written from books they read. Then they can write off that line while inadvertently changing the meaning to fit their own lives.

This strategy, Lifting a Line, will frequently lead the writer in a new direction for the entry. It shows students that there can be more than one starting point. This is especially important for students who write about a championship soccer game and start the entry with waking up in the morning. Lifting a line allows kids to get to the point of what they're trying to write.

The list of strategies can go on and on. There are countless books to inspire writing that work with strategies rather than prompts. As important as teaching some notebook strategies is, however, it is important to allow students to find their own ways of keeping a notebook. I try to limit the number of strategies I teach and then I just let the kids go.

With some strategies under their belts, you will be amazed at how few kids say they have nothing to write about. In addition, many students will have other things on their minds that lead them to "invent" new strategies. As the process of keeping a notebook becomes more familiar, students will write in ways that make sense for their lives. Some students might capture conversations or keep little bits of memorabilia to launch a memory. As your workshop continues through the year, it's important to stop and ask writers how they are keeping their notebooks. Do they notice a pattern in the way they write? Is there a strategy hidden in there that they can teach the class?

From Considerations to Expectations

An important part of planning to use notebooks is preparing for the barrage of "what-ifs" students will ask. As my childhood soccer coach would say, the best defense is a good offense … be prepared. With notebooks, students are going to want direction—a lot of direction. Actually, if a ten-year-old really wants to avoid writing, she or he will revert to the old routine: I don't know how; I don't get it; I don't remember anything. Even if a child is not that overtly obstinate, a few guidelines keep even the best students focused and on task.

At first, I handed students a list of ten expectations I had for them during writing workshop. It worked like a charm, and they kept this list in their writing folders. As the years have gone by, I have changed the rules, adding a few and taking out a few. More recently, I added what students can expect from me. This was a twist to the old do-as-I-say teacher routine. I want students to know that I, too, am working during writing workshop. My work looks different; my main purpose is to help them be better writers.

Figure 2–12 shows a chart of expectations I have in my writing workshop for both the students and myself. I give this to students and parents so we're all clear on who is doing what.

My expectations for writer's workshop extend to the notebook. I encourage teachers to consider these expectations as a starting place. Knowing your community and school will make you the expert in establishing appropriate expectations for your students, as well as yourself.

Figure 2–12   Notebook Expectations

Students are expected to ...	Students can depend on the teacher to ...
write daily in their notebooks at school and at home three times a week (minimum).	provide time each day for students to write during writing workshop.
"find" topics for their notebook writing from their life, from reading, and from natural curiosity. Students are expected to make decisions about their writing topics on a daily basis.	teach writing strategies as ways to discover writing topics. Teachers will also confer with students to help nudge their thinking and writing when students get stuck.
try strategies from the mini-lesson before continuing with their own work for the day.	teach a mini-lesson each day to teach students how to be better writers.
fold over any entry they deem too personal to share with the teacher. (Students may not staple, glue, or tape this page shut.) Any folded-over entries the teacher cannot read will not be considered an entry toward their required number per week.	respect the folded entries. The teacher will respect the privacy of the writer unless there is reason to believe the student is being hurt by someone, is going to hurt someone, or is going to hurt him- or herself.
respect the integrity of the notebook by taking care of it and having it in class every day. Students will respect other notebooks by only reading entries they are invited to read by the author.	have his or her notebook in class on a daily basis. The teacher will also share some of his or her writing throughout the year to establish that she or he too is a writer. Teachers will not lose notebooks they collect, write all over entries in red ink, or spill coffee on them.
practice what they know about conventional spelling and grammar. Entries must be legible.	teach rules of spelling and grammar that will enhance student writing. Teachers will recognize that the notebook is a place to practice new conventions and words and to master conventions and words students already know.
discover how writing can enrich their lives.	discover how his or her life is enriched by the writing of each student.

This list is a starting point. Of course, you don't want to overwhelm children with rule upon rule upon rule. As I review and edit my expectations from year to year, I ask myself: What will students be expected to *do* in the notebook? How often? With what level of "correctness"? How will we (the writer and teacher) respect the privacy of each individual writer in class? What is my ultimate goal and how will I go about directing students toward that end?

Be careful to select or create only the most essential expectations for your students. Keep in mind the most basic goal of the notebook: for students to be independent writers. Expectations need to be the safety net kids fall back on to keep them moving toward this goal. Children need boundaries, and they need to test those boundaries. Consider the expectations as a set of boundaries clarifying the line between student and teacher, and establishing the students' responsibility to write.

You will likely have students write about abuse or about wanting to hurt another student. It's our job to make sure we check the folded-over entries, especially if we see changes in demeanor or radical friendship changes. Then follow your school's policy for reporting these kinds of instances. At times I've checked the folded-over pages to find nothing more than "I'm mad at so and so" or some unsavory language the student used. I have chosen to respect that the page was folded and leave it at that. I do not, however, count folded-over pages toward the notebook grade. This helps to prevent children from folding over all of the entries, leaving me with nothing by which to monitor their writing progress.

Just as we all have students who struggle with reading or math, we'll also have those who struggle with writing. But just as we celebrate when their reading improves or when they finally understand a mathematical concept, the celebration is tenfold when struggling writers finish a writer's notebook.

Chapter 3:

Kneading Notebooks
Expanding Topics and Building Collections of Ideas

My grandmother is a wonderful baker. One of my most cherished memories from childhood is the first time we made bread together. We got up at the crack of dawn. Before breakfast, we began mixing the ingredients for this homemade delight. The conversation, as it's been retold to me over and over, went something like this: "Once we get the dough mixed and kneaded, we'll put it to bed," said Grandma.

"We have to kneel on the dough?" I asked rubbing my knees.

"No, dear," my grandmother replied patiently, "We need to *knead* it. We'll roll it and rub it, pat it and squish it, we'll move it around and mix it up until it's soft and smooth. It's one thing to get these ingredients mixed together. It's another thing entirely to get them to blend in and work together. The taste and smell of bread is only as good as the kneading that came before it."

As my grandmother showed me how to knead, our hands finding a common rhythm, each with our own glob of dough, I said, "But this is hard and my hands are hurting."

"Stick with it," she always said, "It'll be worth it in the end."

The bread was delicious, as always, and to this day I can't—I won't—use a bread machine.

Kneading bread is a lot like working a topic. The notebooks our students keep are filled with the ingredients for good writing. But will they mix well? Will they blend in and work together? Even if the answer is no because your students keep a notebook like a journal—they write in it and that's the end of it—your students' work will still improve. Their writing will get better.

But kneading the notebook—working a topic, expanding it, and blending different entries together—can create a piece of writing, and a process approach to writing that is unimaginable. My students claim it's like magic—after working so long in their notebooks (kneading a topic) their drafts just seem to fall out of their heads. Of course, it's not magic at all. It's hard work, and it's a process worth showing your students.

Finding Patterns

Recently I had a parent conference with Nate's mom. Before she left, she turned to tell me just one more thing. "I don't know whether I should thank you or not for teaching Nate the value of writing," she started, half jokingly. "Really? Why?" I asked. She responded with this story:

"The other day Nate asked me if we had PowerPoint on our computer and how to bring it up. He then proceeded to write a six-slide presentation, with all of the bells and whistles, as to why his father and I should let him have a paintball gun. He even ended it with a conclusion that wrapped up his points!"

She laughed and smiled, as she shook her head. "I guess we should gear up for written arguments that are high tech."

After the conference, I went back to Nate's notebook . . . just to see. Yes, it is plagued with paintball entries. I am reminded just how often writers write in patterns, if only we took the time to reread and look for them. Sometimes the patterns are not well developed through the pieces; however, if a student is keeping a notebook, topic patterns will emerge in his or her writing.

Finding patterns in their writing is a useful skill for writers. It helps them see what they are (subconsciously) thinking about. By recognizing patterns students can more easily figure out what they want to write about when working toward a finished piece. I usually have students work in pairs as we begin this lesson.

"I've been thinking," I begin, "What do you write about?"

"All sorts of stuff," Matthew replies.

"But what kinds of patterns are emerging in your writing?"

"I thought patterns are for math," Tori thinks aloud.

"Last night," I continue, "I was thinking about my writing patterns. When I first started keeping a notebook, I wrote a lot about school, my sister, and my (then) husband. However, as my life changed—my sister moved away, I had a child, I got a divorce—my writing patterns changed. Now I write more about my son and the wacky things he sometimes does. I keep political commentaries about what is happening with education nationwide, and I write a lot about plants."

"You like to garden," Matthew adds.

"You're right, and I use a lot of gardening references and metaphors in my notebook. I hadn't realized I was doing that until I reread my notebook."

By now some students are anticipating the directive for today's workshop, and start leafing through their notebooks.

"Today, I want you to take some time out from writing to reread your notebook. Try to notice any ideas or themes that seem to keep popping up. It may be a person who tends to be in many entries, or a hobby. Feel free to write in the margins, highlight, or fold the corner of pages over to track these patterns. Take time to read carefully and give thoughtful consideration to the question, What is (are) your writing pattern(s)? At the end of the workshop, you'll have time to meet with a partner and discuss what you discovered."

And off they go. Some students have trouble with this, so I don't start conferring until I'm sure everyone is rereading their notebooks. I then begin conferences to help clarify directions and to give more specific help in identifying a pattern.

As my life has changed, so has my writing. We can expect the same for our students. Unfortunately, we won't be around for all of our students' life changes. This is why teaching them strategies for writing is so important. Showing our students that they do write in patterns and helping them recognize these patterns and how they change over time is developing a life skill for them as writers. It is a skill they can depend on for their whole lives.

These next entries are all from Jared's notebook, collected over a one-month period. As you read them, notice the emerging themes (patterns). Some ideas will be evident, others not. I keep these particular samples to share with my students as a mini-lesson on how to find patterns within their writing.

●◆ 2-11

How do you feel about Jean Bennay Ramsey, Ms. Colorado was murdered. Why do you think her dad hired a defense lawyer if his daughter was murdered? Why aren't the parents talking to the police? Who do you think killed her?

●◆ 2-12

Grandpa Gene
My grandpa died a year ago. He died in his sleep so there was no pain at least I think. My grandma called and left a message on my recorder that said Geney call me immediately. He called and found out Grandpa was dead. He came down and told us what happened. I didn't know what I should do. I didn't know what I felt—somewhere between mad, happy, or sad, maybe all of them at the same time.

2-25

Water

Water is a strange word. What does it mean? What does land mean? What does time mean? Is there ever enough time? How much more time do I have left in my time? Do you know what's mean and stinks, abortion when you kill the baby inside you. It probably doesn't get another life. Like the bombs that are being set in the gay bars and abortion clinics. It has probably been the same person judging other people. You might not like what they do or did, but that doesn't give you the right to just go off and kill them. Where do you think the next bomb will go off if there will be another one?

2-27

People, Time

People never have enough—do aliens ever have enough time, if there are aliens? Is an alien just like a mythical creature? Have they ever existed? Will they ever? Do you believe in aliens? I kind of do and kind of don't. I kind of hope there isn't any because if there is will they try to take over our planet like in the movies?

3-5

One day I was walking through the mall and saw some fake toenails. Guess what happened? They were selling them by twelves. Are they for aliens or something? Maybe ten for the toes and two for the fingers. Geez, it isn't like one of them is going to fall off, you glue them on.

3-11

People

People, geez, why are they always so stupid? They can never find their shoes. The reason I don't like humans is because of the movies Mars Attacks and Independence Day, because aliens aren't like that. I would know, I am one!

3-11

Moon

The moon is awake always 24 hours a day 7 days a week 31
days a month and so on. It is always shining as bright as a
mother's eyes when she sees her new born baby. It's always
awake but shining on the other side.

As you read through these entries, certain patterns just pop out.
Aliens are definitely on Jared's mind. He's struggling with the idea of whether
or not they are real, what they may look like, and if they are mean or not.
He's also thinking a lot about death, natural and otherwise. There are a lot of
feelings he's associating with death—anger and sadness—while also trying to
understand why humans would kill others. He can't seem to find a good reason
for them to do so.

Jared also talks a bit about time and family relationships. Did you notice
he brought up the relationships between parents and children three different
times … with Jon Benet Ramsey, his father and grandparents, and in "Moon,"
between the mother and baby.

From one month's worth of notebook entries, Jared has a lot to choose
from when deciding on a topic for his next published piece of writing. His topics
also lean toward a variety of genres: editorial (Jon Benet Ramsey piece), poetry
("Moon,"), and persuasion ("People," "Toenails," "Time").

Reading Jared's work, you might wonder if he is gifted. No, Jared was not
in the gifted program at school. It is typical work for students who write regularly.
I think one of the key factors that makes Jared's work so interesting is that he has
found a voice. You can see how this little boy thinks. And you can tell from the
samples that this all came from the same child. He has a writing style.

When I stop by to confer with Jared, I don't know his patterns yet,
although from reading his notebook regularly, I have a good idea of the kinds
of things he tends to write about. Jared is a floor buff—he would rather work
on the floor than at his desk. During writing workshop, my requirement is that
students find someplace to write on their own. Jared is sitting against a wall near
the back of the classroom.

"Jared, can you take a moment to stop and talk?" I ask as I kneel down
next to him.

"Yup. You know, finding patterns is getting easier for me. It's almost like I'm thinking of writing in patterns without knowing it," he says.

"Really? What do you mean?" I'm a bit taken aback that he jumped into this conference in this way. Jared usually waits for me to ask a question.

"Well, look, I write a lot about world events—Jon Benet Ramsey, the abortion clinic bombings, and I write about death—those two plus my grandpa. Of course, I also like aliens."

"You have a lot going on in your notebook, Jared. The trick now is to narrow your thinking down to one topic for a writing project," I reply.

"I think I'm going to write about aliens," he says matter-of-factly.

"Really? Why?" I must admit I'm disappointed at first, because I think he has other important topics to write about.

"Well, it will be more fun than writing about the other things. I think I wrote about those to get them off my mind. But I like to think about aliens. I'll write about aliens."

Out of the mouths of babes: he likes aliens. He knows he's going to spend some time on this writing project, so he might as well write what he likes. This really is a key to keeping students engaged in their own writing. They need to buy in to what they're writing. If I forced Jared to write about death or family relationships, he'd do it, but not as enthusiastically as he'll write about aliens. Ultimately, the choice is his. He accomplished what I set out to do—he learned to reread for patterns and make a writing decision.

These next samples by Courtney are much different. They come from the beginning of the year. She writes with typically surface-level ideas, and hasn't yet developed the ability to think as deeply about her topics as Jared has. However, as patterns emerge, anyone reading her entries can definitely get a sense of who Courtney is and what is important to her.

8/19 Having a Twin

Having a twin is good but bad in a way. Everybody says, "Are you a twin?" I think it is obvious that we're twins, we look exactly alike. Lots of people ask if we wear the same clothes. I always say, NO.

➤ 8/19 Twin Switch

One time Caroline and I were late for pre-school, so our teachers came out and grabbed us [out of carpool]. The thing was, they grabbed the wrong one. Caroline's teacher grabbed me and my teacher grabbed Caroline. We didn't tell the teachers because we were too shy. That is one of my favorite memories.

➤ 9/03 Softball

I have played softball for a long time. I've been on All Stars 4 times. I have 14 trophies—I like to collect them. I have shelves of them. I LOVE SOFTBALL it is my favorite sport. My dream is to play for the Georgia Bulldogs. I sometimes like to brag about how good I am. My sister gets mad. I am better [than her] I think. I think my mom and dad think the same but won't say anything. I love playing pitcher.

➤ 9/8 Basketball

I had a basketball game and we won 18 to 9. My [basketball] coach is my softball coach. I think we might make it to the championships. There are 7 girls on my team. Caroline plays too. Basketball is my second favorite sport. I usually play it in the winter and play softball in the other seasons.

➤ 9/8 The Moondogs

The Moondogs is a team that I was on when I was 9. I was the main pitcher. Softball is my favorite sport. I always try to do my best, and it always pays off too. This year I was on the Allstars team. I love everything about softball. My favorite picture is of me pitching. Our team won the championship. We got two trophies and a medal. After the Moondogs I started Allstars with the same coaches. I really like them. I also got them for basketball. They LOVE me. Caroline didn't make it. Caroline felt bad and didn't want to talk about it.

9/9 When I Moved

*I moved to Snellville when I was 7. I thought I would never again
have friends. I lived in Lawrenceville and had three teachers.
Ever since I moved I wonder if they remember me. I made lots of
friends to my surprise. I play with all of my friend a lot.*

9/10 Leaving Collins Hill Park (Softball)

*I thought I would never play softball again. I thought I would
never see my softball coaches again, but of course I did. I saw all
of them at Allstars. I saw all of them except Coach Tim. I wonder
if he remembers me. He worked me harder than the other
players because he knew how good I was. My best friend was
on the team. I know she remembers me because we always see
each other at Allstars.*

There are some obvious patterns: having a twin, softball, and AllStars.
Courtney mentions these over and over again. Yet she hasn't developed any of
them in a more meaningful way. Her topics are prime for *kneading* into something
more significant. Also, there are glimpses of insecurity. She wonders if people will
remember her—teachers, coaches, friends. She only moved across town, but her
fears are as valid as if she moved across the country.

In this situation, at the beginning of the year, I had collected the
notebooks for assessment (see Chapter 7), and made notes of possible patterns for
each child. I do this early in the year because I know some children will need more
support than others, and I didn't know these writers yet. I needed the backup of
my notes to help me guide students in a meaningful way.

"Hey, Court," I sit down in the desk next to hers, "can we talk?"

"Ummm, sure," she says as she finishes reading the entry she is on, folds
the corner over, and writes "pattern" on it.

"I see you're finding some patterns in your writing," I begin the conference.

"Yep," she replies.

"Tell me about what you're finding." I'm having to guide this conference
more than I'd like, but I'm not taking over—I keep giving general statements for
her to respond to and mark direction for our conversation.

"Well, I write a lot about softball. I also noticed Caroline is in my entries a lot," she responds while flipping aimlessly through her notebook, as if looking for the answers.

"Great!" I respond. "I read your notebook this weekend and noticed some of the same patterns. Did you notice how you wonder if people will remember you? You mention that a couple of times."

"Yeah. But I think softball is better."

I focus this conversation a bit more. "Courtney, you are welcome to write about softball, but I want to warn you about a trap writers sometimes fall into. Sometimes we choose a topic soooo big, that there is no good way to write about it."

"Is softball too big?" she asks.

"I think you need to spend some time thinking about a part of softball you might want to explain."

"Do you mean like a position or one game?" she asks.

"Those are two good ideas for narrowing the topic. It seems to me that you have a lot of softball memories."

"Yes," she says confidently.

"I would concentrate on that and look for or think about memories that you could write more about in your notebook."

This is how it evolves—children moving from their everyday writing to writing something meaningful. It starts with a glimpse, a pattern, and then grows into something bigger. When working with notebooks and urging children to do their own thinking and writing, this kind of work becomes typical, expected, and ongoing.

From Pattern to Piece: Developing a Topic

Patterns in students' notebooks arise over time. Because each student will write from his or her own experiences, patterns are going to be different. After students learn to reread their notebooks and identify patterns, I ask them to choose one that they would like to spend some time thinking about, and then write a published piece.

I am careful to refer to their writing as a published piece or a finished piece rather than a story. Not all students will be writing a story. Some students, like Jared, have patterns that lend themselves to other genres beyond the typical narrative. As children become more immersed with their notebooks and working with different genres, how to write their pieces will become as important to them as choosing their topics.

Strategies for Expanding Ideas and Collecting Materials Around a Topic

After students choose a topic, they need time to focus on that topic before beginning a draft outside the notebook. This process takes a different amount of time, every time, for each student. All of them start by rereading the entries that relate to the chosen pattern or topic. Many kids then write a general entry about where their thinking is going with this topic. This is an important step; they are merging thoughts collected over time. Sometimes, by this point, nine- and ten-year-olds have an idea about the direction of their writing.

Many writing experts say kids should spend time just collecting around one topic. Some topics lend themselves to that, but some don't. Sometimes students have the patience to do that, sometimes they don't. In my humble opinion based on my years in the classroom, the amount of time students spend on collecting around a topic varies and should be flexible. Some writing pieces are more urgent than others. If a child wants to write a poem for her sick grandfather, she isn't going to spend a week thinking about her grandfather in order to write the poem. The energy in the piece is generated from a life circumstance—her grandpa is sick and she wants to write a poem for him. Go with that energy.

On the other hand, if the topic is a childhood memory that a student wants to make into a picture book, he or she may spend some time thinking about that memory in different ways, trying to get details from different perspectives in order to write a well-developed story. This time, there is no urgency in the timing.

When I say *collecting around a topic*, I'm referring to a process that some writers use after selecting a main idea. Writers spend time researching, thinking, and wondering about a particular idea. This is different from what kids are doing in their notebooks on a regular basis, because this process is a focused study on one topic within their notebooks. Again, it's a time for teachers to introduce strategies to knead these ideas into writing.

I have students keep these strategies in the front section of their notebooks, with other entries that they may want to reread and refer to as they begin to write. Students are not drafting yet. We're still in the notebook, but the purpose of the notebook has changed slightly. Now, instead of writing about all sorts of things on any given day, we're using specific strategies to think about a specific topic. Some students may want more organization than this, and they'll use sticky notes to mark the pages with the topic's or strategy's name. Or they might add it to the table of contents to reference later in the year.

Multiple Entries for a Topic

Collecting entries around a topic is important to help writers think through their pieces. In the "writing steps" people adhere to in the textbooks, this is referred to as brainstorming. It seems scattered but it leads to deeper, more thoughtful writing when students do go to draft. It's easy for teachers to get caught up in making rules for how many entries students need around a topic in their notebooks or how long a student must collect information. I know, I've been in that dark pit before, when I needed to know or have proof that kids were thinking and to show students I was serious about it. But I found that students lose their enthusiasm and energy for topics the more I make them do before drafting. It's a balancing act that we get the feel for over time. Some students need to collect more than others. Some topics gain energy with collecting while others wane.

By teaching students that this is a process and the strategies are there to help, we can help them make decisions about how many more entries or how much time they spend on a topic before writing. Students must develop that inner alarm that goes off when it's time to draft. When it's time, it's time.

How do I know when to introduce one of these new strategies? I ask myself, what do most of my students need at this point to help them with their writing? I say most, because not all students will need a particular strategy at a particular time. Also, I don't always know exactly what they need. Sometimes I am stumped, and I'm not above making stuff up as I go along. Many times we have that teacher's intuition, but because no one said it in a book, we don't follow it. I'm saying it now. Follow your intuition when you have an idea. Your students will help you mold it into a good strategy.

Three by Threes

I find that my students struggle to add details to their writing. Have you ever read a piece of student writing that has absolutely no details in it? Or a piece that has more adjectives than nouns or verbs? The paradox of children's writing is that they get so caught up in writing long pieces (or short ones), they forget to envision the piece. If a reader is to be able to see the story in his or her mind, then someone has to create that image, and that someone is the writer. Three-Word Phrases in Three Minutes is a quick notebook exercise to help students begin to see a topic, to envision parts of it.

Here is how I introduce Three-Word Phrases in Three Minutes: "Today, we're going to do a quick writer's exercise. It's a strategy you can use whenever you're stuck in your writing. I need someone to choose a noun."

"School," someone says.

"Okay, write 'school' at the top of the first clean page of your notebook. Remember to date the page. Now, I'm going to give you three minutes, and I want you to write as many three-word phrases about school as you can. Who can think of a quick example to get us started?"

Some hands go up, and I call on Kelsey. "A long recess," she says.

Giggles escape from around the room, but it's a good example. "Good job, Kelsey. It's three words, it's a phrase, and it's about school. It works. I'll time you, get ready, get set, go!" And for three minutes they write.

This example is a great one. It focuses the subject. School is a huge topic. If a child were going to write about school, the story could be never-ending. Using this strategy, some students might find a focus for their topics based on their phrases. Others will find wonderful similes to add or images to create.

Once the class has finished the three-minute exercise and shared some responses, I ask them to use this strategy with a topic or pattern they have discovered in their notebooks (Figure 3–1).

Figure 3–1 *Expanding Topics Strategy: Three-Word Phrases in Three Minutes*

How: Students select a topic to focus on as they write. For three minutes, they list as many three-word phrases about the topic as they possibly can.

Why? This strategy helps students focus on parts of a larger topic. By limiting the phrases to three words, students are forced to be specific and choosy about what they write. It's also a good exercise for building fluency because a timed writing requires quick thinking.

Extensions: This strategy can be used for anything a writer wants to think more deeply about: a character, a setting, a feeling. It can also be used across the curriculum to help students isolate important information. For example, in social studies I might ask the kids to do this with a topic such as the American Revolution or magnetism in science.

Write from Another Point of View

Writing from another point of view is a great strategy for childhood memories or events in students' lives. I share these two entries from my notebook on the overhead.

✏ Mikey and the Muffin

I had just baked some fresh blueberry muffins at Mikey's request. As they cooled, I read When You Give a Moose a Muffin. Afterward, we sat down to eat. The phone rang and it was a good friend, so I started to talk to her. Mikey turned from a sweet adorable three-year-old to an obstinate tantrum-throwing toddler. He started to drop bits of his muffin on the floor. I excused myself from my conversation long enough to tell him to stop. Then he picked up his muffin and threw it across the kitchen. Again I stopped my conversation and told him, "Go pick that up. We don't throw food." "NO!" came his response loud and clear. I quickly got off the phone and the battle of picking up the muffin was on.

✏ Muffin Battle—Mikey's Point of View as Imagined by His Mother

I love the smell of these muffins, too bad they're too hot to eat. Oh yeah, I get to cuddle with mommy and a book while they cool. Hey, this book is about muffins too! I love spending time with my mommy. It's time to eat. I take a bite—yummy! The phone rings. Geez, she's on the phone again. I'll just start putting some of this muffin on the floor. She'll remember I'm here. She just yelled at me. I'll show her. I throw the muffin across the room. HA! I'm not picking it up. Oh no, she's off the phone. This did the trick, but now I'm going to have to hold my ground to keep her off the phone.

After reading the two entries to the kids, I say, "In the first entry I'm mad at Mikey for throwing food. Then in the next entry I stop to think about why he might have done it. I don't really know, I never asked him, but this is what I think he might have thought. Now I have a better idea of what was happening. So when I go to write, I'll think about how he's trying to find ways to keep me off the phone" (Figure 3–2).

Figure 3–2 *Expanding Topics Strategy: Writing from Another Point of View*

How: I start off by telling students a story about something my son did or said. I then retell the story from his point of view—imagining his thoughts and ideas about what happened. I end it with this question: Has it ever happened to you that your sibling or parent remembers the same event as you but in a different way? Hands will go up. Then I direct the students to try writing their narratives from a different person's point of view. What details change? How does seeing the story through other eyes help you see more of what to write?

Why? Children tend to write things from their points of view. It takes teaching and time to help them see things from other people's perspectives. Being able to write from a different viewpoint opens the writing to details, emotions, and events that may have been forgotten.

Extensions: Read books that give different points of view in the story. Some great example texts are: *The Pain and the Great One* by Judy Blume (1995), *Hey, Little Ant* by Phillip Hoose and Hannah Hoose (1998), and *The True Story of the Three Little Pigs* by Jon Scieszka (1995).

Students write about an incident based on what they thought happened. Then they choose someone else who was there, and write the story from that person's perspective. If possible, they interview or talk with the other person first. By thinking about how someone else saw the situation, students often reveal insights that may not have originally occurred to them. A great book for introducing this is the classic *The Pain and The Great One* by Judy Blume (1995).

Favorite Collection

At our school, the media specialist has a special cabinet for students to showcase their favorite collections. Kids sign up for different weeks and then display everything from cars to teddy bears.

This same concept can be applied to writing. Students think about what aspects of their topics they would display. So if someone's topic were a story about his dad, the child might make a list of things to put in the display case that would show others about his dad. After making the list, the student would reflect on why the items are important symbols of who his dad is as a person. Some of these details or symbols would enrich and help develop the story about his dad (Figure 3–3).

Figure 3–3 *Expanding Topics Strategy: Favorite Collection*

How: Ask the students, "If we were to go to a museum that had an exhibit about [pause for dramatic effect] *me*, what do you think would be displayed?" Students of mine often answer: books, pictures of Mikey, cookie recipes, DVDs of my favorite movies, rubbermate pencils, my coffee mugs that change with the seasons, etc. I then ask the students, why? Naturally, they have a reason for every one of those objects, as they reflect things that are important to me. Children can do the same thing for a character or person in a narrative. In the notebook, they create a list of objects to be exhibited in a museum collection, then discuss what will be there and why.

Why? This strategy requires writers to think more deeply about who they are writing about in their piece. It often leads to putting in details that allow the reader to infer information. This also helps students develop and enrich their stories.

Extensions: This strategy can be used across the curriculum. What would be in an exhibit of the Boston Massacre?

Interviews

Interviewing people is a common strategy that professional writers use. Newspaper reporters interview witnesses or people who know a lot about the topic to get "both sides" of a story. Although this strategy naturally lends itself to nonfiction work, it can also be done with fiction and poetry.

Students who are writing fiction don't see how this strategy applies to them, but it's crucial that they learn it. I've read countless fictional stories containing multiple characters and no character development that go on for five pages ... or more.

Don Graves and Nancie Atwell both talk about developing characters with questions. Authors need to know their characters so they can tell the reader about them. When young students write in first person, they know the character inside out because it's them. But, when they begin making up stories, it's important that they take some time to develop and think about the main character(s) and ask questions like what does the character look like? How old is the character? What is the character's worst habit? Best habit? What would the character never do? What does the character do when she or he is upset? The list can go on. The more questions they can ask, the better their characters will be. Doing this thinking in their notebooks, before they go to draft, is especially helpful.

Figure 3–4 *Expanding Topics Strategy: Interviews*

How: Students decide whom they might want to interview and the questions they want to ask. Often it's helpful for kids to think about what they want to know and ask questions about that. It may seem obvious to us, but not to a ten-year-old. Students then arrange a time to interview the person and take notes on their responses.

Why? Nine- and ten-year-olds don't realize that there might be more information about a story or person that they don't know. It doesn't occur to them to ask a parent what they remember about the trip to Disney. Or to ask their grandma about their grandpa who passed away. This strategy helps students realize that writers talk to people about their topics. Ideas come from all sorts of sources—even from parents!

Extensions: Students can certainly practice this strategy by interviewing each other and doing a quick-write about their partner. Students can also use this strategy to ask thoughtful questions when writing to an author or a foreign exchange student.

Interviews can help writers find out what other people think. If Jared were going to write a piece on aliens, it would be helpful for him to find out whether other kids believe in aliens, what scientists think about their existence, or what kinds of stories have already been written about aliens. Sometimes interviews lead kids to research. Again, it all goes toward developing a better story.

K-N-T Chart

A favorite strategy of many teachers is the K-N-T chart. K-N-T stands for: What I *Know*, What I *Need* to Know, and What I *Think*. Students use this graphic organizer to help them see their thinking. Students draw this chart in their notebooks and fill it in as they work on their topics. It may take them one writing session or several, depending on the topic (Figure 3–5).

Figure 3–5 *Expanding Topics Strategy: KNT Chart*

K-N-T (Know—Need to Know—What I Think) Chart

How: Students create a three-column chart in their notebooks with the headings K-N-T. They then fill in the chart using phrases and key ideas. This chart is usually done in a note-taking format. Students can then look at their notes to highlight ideas or thoughts they want to include in their writing.

Why? When students have to collect research or read about a topic before writing, this strategy helps them keep track of their thinking. In addition, it allows writers to learn more about their topics before writing. Many times kids think they have to go from notebook to draft without any other work. This chart gives them permission to spend a bit of time learning more about a topic they're interested in.

Extensions: This is actually an extension of a K-W-L chart. It can be used across the curriculum, especially when students need to do research.

Jared's topic about aliens lends itself to a chart like this. It gives him a quick way to keep notes, especially if he has to do some research. Also, as a student thinks through his or her topic, new questions may come to mind. As you can see in the following chart, the idea of aliens from outer space begins to mingle with illegal immigration in the United States (Figure 3–6).

Figure 3–6 *Jared's Alien Chart*

Know	Need to Know	My Thinking
• Aliens are in the movies and destroy Earth a lot. • Aliens are from outer space. • In books, aliens can look like humans.	• Does everyone believe in aliens? • Do aliens exist? • Where in outer space do they come from? • Have aliens ever really come to Earth? • How can an alien be illegal? Are there laws that prevent aliens from coming to Earth? If so, how do aliens know?	• Everyone does *not* believe in aliens. A lot of my friends don't. • Mrs. Greer, the librarian, said alien books are science*fiction*—she said fiction twice. I don't think she's a believer. • I heard a phrase on the news about *illegal* aliens. • Maybe they're breaking the law and don't know it.

Listing the Possibilities

Listing the Possibilities is a similar strategy to the launching strategy Writing from a List. Actually, it's the same strategy, but with a different purpose. Just as before, students make a list focused on a topic. This time, however, the purpose isn't to generate different kinds of entries like the best/worst lists. The purpose of this strategy is to help narrow down a larger topic or to think more deeply about a focused topic. For example, students often want to write about a sport, like Courtney did. She loves softball. Here is how a list about softball might help her focus her writing.

Softball memories:

1. Playing first base
2. Playing pitcher
3. Playing on the All-Star team
4. Playing on the same team as Caroline
5. Having to switch teams because I moved
6. Having the same coaches for basketball and softball
7. Dreaming to play on the Georgia Bulldogs one day
8. The time I hit a homerun four times in one game
9. When I sprained my arm and couldn't play
10. When my team won 18 to 9.

All of these "memories" can be found in bits and pieces in her earlier notebook entries. By creating a list, she can think of each memory as a story on its own. Writing from this list will give Courtney a better focus for her final piece (Figure 3–7).

Figure 3-7   *Expanding Topics Strategy: Listing the Possibilities*

How: This strategy is much like the list students make when beginning the notebook. The topic of the list is whatever they have chosen to write about. Students list memories, events, equipment, places, etc., that relate to the topic. The list shows the topic broken down, and the writer can choose a part of it to write about. This works best with topics that are too big to write about in one story.

Why? When students have a large topic, like Six Flags, they try to write about all of it and end up listing what happened. It's important for writers to narrow down a topic to something that is manageable. The list is an easy way for kids to break the topic down without even realizing they're doing it.

Caution: Warn your students to be careful not to overuse this strategy. Like any strategy, it loses its luster and becomes mundane if used exclusively or too much. The key to keeping the strategy fresh is using it periodically.

Time to Draft

There comes a time when writers must start a draft. Just like some bakers who don't let their dough rise enough or who allow it to rise too long, some writers want to draft *now* and others would stay in their notebooks forever. Part of being a good writer is like being a good baker, you need to know when the dough is ready.

Drafting is a lot like pouring the kneaded dough into a bread pan—the thoughts are well mixed and ready to rise. By the time students have kept a notebook, reflected, found a pattern, and collected entries around a chosen topic, they are *ready* to write. My students are always surprised at this the first time they go through the process. It takes them a while to realize how much work they have already done before the draft takes shape.

Because this is a book about the writer's notebook, I want to clarify how I use the notebook while students are drafting. It isn't necessarily the right way, it's just my way: I don't use the notebook at all.

Students in my class leave their notebooks and use yellow legal-pads to draft their longer pieces. We do this for several reasons. First, drafts are meant to be worked on, cut up, added to, and changed. I don't want the notebook cut up and it's hard to add to it when there is a new entry right behind the story.

Second, I don't want students copying directly from their notebooks. They leave their notebooks for a day or two while they write their drafts—from their heads. With all the collecting and prewriting they have done in the notebook, this is not a difficult task.

Third, we'll use the notebook to try out revision strategies for the draft. The revision strategies presented in the following chapters are tried out in the notebook, *then* the students choose the best revisions to add to the draft. This prevents the need for multiple drafts and time wasted rewriting the good parts. Besides, kids hate doing that. Writing is hard enough without creating obstacles that don't need to be there.

Chapter 4:

When Writers Read

I learned how to write from writers. I didn't know any personally, but I read. —Cynthia Rylant

I still remember meeting my mentor teacher, Rhonda Mumaw, for student teaching. Her room was filled with books, her students told me their favorite subject was writing, and the atmosphere was more like a home than a classroom. It was exciting, and looked nothing like anything I had experienced before. I hated (at that time) to read, I avoided the children's literature course in college like the plague, and my favorite subject was math.

Luckily for me, I was open to learning everything I could from Rhonda. When I say everything, I mean everything—from loving books and writing to interacting with children in a kind, respectful manner. During my first year of teaching, I regularly drove fifty miles to visit Rhonda and soak up the essence of the kind of teacher I wanted to be someday.

Some of us are fortunate to have mentors available to us at different times in our lives to show us the way. The trick is to know how to learn from them. Students also need mentors. Parents mentor children in attitudes, coaches mentor athletes in sports, and teachers mentor children in learning.

But writers lead a lonely life. They work independently from mind to paper. Sure, they talk about their work with their editors or other confidants, but when push comes to shove, they're on their own. Similarly, when teachers teach writing, we often feel like we're on our own.

Writers have mentors, too. They're right in front of us. Whenever authors are asked for advice on how to write well, their answer is always the same: READ. This is not a difficult battle cry for teachers to follow. But does simply reading make you a better writer? Is there some sort of magic that happens when you've read a certain number of books? Does it matter what kind of books you read? Do cereal boxes count?

When writers read, they take a different stance toward the book than "regular" people do. When we read for pleasure, we get lost in the story and visualize what is happening. Writers do the same thing at times; however, their relationship to other writers is like my relationship with Rhonda. Just as I needed to talk with Rhonda, to visit her classroom, and to notice the big and little things she did to be the kind of teacher I wanted to be, writers need to examine and explore the books they read.

Writers admire other writers. They read to soak up the essence of their favorite authors. They are aware of how characters are being developed, how the words are put together to create a mood, and how the writer's style affects the reader. Writers apply techniques in a certain way to create the best work they can. Children can infer and learn these techniques by studying the writing of what they read in the same way that writers do.

The writer's notebook can support this learning. Students glue in copies of good writing, reflect on different styles of text, and emulate favorite authors— all in the safely saved pages of their notebooks.

This process, which has become known as "reading like a writer," is eloquently described by Katie Wood Ray in her book *Wondrous Words* (1996). She compares reading like a writer to being a seamstress:

> Because my friend is a seamstress, she goes to the mall ... differently than the rest of us who aren't seamstresses. ... While the rest of us mere shoppers are looking only at [dress] sizes and prices, my friend is looking closely at the inseams and stitching. ... She wants to know how what she sees was made, how it was put together. ... You see, my friend's not shopping for clothes, she's shopping for ideas for clothes. (p. 13)

We already do this as teachers—we're constantly looking at the ways children learn, how they keep their knowledge, and how to motivate them further. Which one of us hasn't borrowed an idea from a colleague, tweaked it, and used it in our classrooms?

Using authors as mentors for student writing is a similar process—looking at parts of a text and thinking about what the author did to make the writing work that way. As students use their notebooks to collect their ideas and observations about how other authors write, they begin to see patterns in writing and story structure, to recognize different styles of creating mood and tone, and even to identify their own writing style. The best part about this process is that there are no right or wrong answers, because authors don't always realize all the things they've done in their writing. But students who are purposefully reading to learn about writing can and should be purposeful in what they do when they write.

I was standing in line at a national conference, waiting for Julius Lester to sign my book. I love his writing. *John Henry* (Lester and Pickney 1999) is my favorite picture book, and I use it every year with my students and in most staff development sessions I lead. It's the first book I truly read like a writer, and I've never been the same since. I couldn't wait to meet Mr. Lester and tell him the influence he has had on me as a writer and a teacher. As I waited, anxiously looking ahead, wishing people wouldn't talk so long to him, the woman in front of me began to talk to me.

"Do you know anything about this author?" she asked.

"Julius Lester? Are you kidding? I love his work," I replied, incredulous that she had no idea who he was.

"Oh, then maybe you can help me. I have to introduce him at his next session, but I don't know anything about him."

I launched into a passionate soliloquy about his writing. I told her about *John Henry*, how it's a metaphor for Martin Luther King Jr.'s life, how the writing moves me and my students. I told her about his other books, and as I was talking I heard someone chuckling. I looked over to see that we were standing in front of Julius Lester himself. Grinning from ear to ear, he shook his head and said, "I didn't know I did all that. I just write the books."

Most of our students may not be as gifted as Julius Lester, but they can learn from him and other authors they love to read. As I have tinkered with this process, my students and I have developed a ritual. When I come home from a conference, I lug an extra suitcase I bought just to cart home all the books and paraphenalia I found. I take it to school the next day and we have a little ceremony … the unpacking ritual.

I gather the students around me with this big suitcase in the middle and, as they wait eagerly to see what's inside, I slowly and quite dramatically unzip it. Books, pencils, bookmarks, notepads, and all sorts of free stuff that I collected spill onto the floor. Together, we unpack the suitcase, looking at all the books and trinkets, finding places to put all of this stuff, as I tell the stories of how I gathered it all. Students listen to hear if I met their favorite author or poet, eager to connect their images of authors to knowing what they're like in real life. Best of all, students marvel at the selection of new books as I unpack them.

Reading like a writer, for craft or structure, is very much the same. Writers like to "unpack" the books they love. They like to take a second look at the text, explore the details, ask themselves: How did they do that? Film fans want to know how the special effects were created for *Lord of the Rings*; computer users want to know how the ipod and all of its accessories work. We play, we examine the insides, we unpack things bit by bit—until we understand.

How to write a great first line of a piece had been a mystery to me for a long time. The hardest part about getting started, after finding a topic, is writing that first sentence. It has to grab the reader's attention. It's a lot of pressure to come up with a "grabber lead." I began to collect first lines from books I loved. I studied them. Using these first lines as a mentor text, I got better at writing grabber leads. I share this "study" approach with my students in the form of two strategies, Grabber Leads and Try Ten.

With Grabber Leads, we begin by finding the best possible leads from other authors to guide us. We research the leads of favorite stories and make a list in our notebooks of maybe ten leads. We then discuss what grabs our attention about these leads.

I read an example from *Charlotte's Web*: "'Where's Papa going with that ax?' said Fern to her mother as they were setting the table for breakfast" (White 1974, p. 1). Then I say, "That is the first sentence of the much-loved children's classic *Charlotte's Web*. What did E. B. White do that grabs our attention?" The students answer readily.

"He uses a question."

"He gets me thinking—why would a dad have an ax? What is he going to do with it?"

Most chapter books don't start with a weapon. This makes the reader think something exciting might happen. "So, from just this one lead, we have learned that questions make good beginnings. Grabber leads need to make the reader wonder and want to read more. And grabber leads may say something unexpected to keep the reader reading." I go on to ask the students to choose ten books or other texts (magazines, newspapers, etc.) from the library and write down the lead sentences in their notebooks. Later, they will spend some time with partners discussing the leads on their lists. Students write down what they think makes these leads great starts to stories (Figure 4–1).

Figure 4–1   *Read to Write Strategy: Grabber Leads*

How: Begin by discussing the importance of the first line of a story. This is known as the lead. Tell students it's one of the most important sentences in the entire piece because it has to grab the reader's attention. If the first sentence (or two) doesn't get the reader's attention, the reader may stop reading. That is bad; writers want people to read their work.

Share a few lead sentences from different sources. I try to include some fiction and nonfiction during this lesson. Discuss with students how the lead grabbed your attention. Students then can look in their own books or other resources in the room to find some grabber leads.

Students will need time to share their findings with a partner and then with the class. As students share, make a chart to hang in the classroom.

Why? By looking at other writers' work in books or articles, students can begin to think about different ways to start their own writing.

Extension: This mini-lesson can be adapted to discuss transition sentences or topic sentences in the middle of a piece. I use a passage from *Maniac Magee* (Spinelli 1990) and current articles from *Time for Kids* or *National Geographic Explorer* as examples.

After students have had time to explore leads on their own and with a partner, we come together as a class to create an anchor chart based on their research (Figure 4–2).

Figure 4–2 *Grabber Leads Anchor Chart*

Fiction

•❖*Charlotte's Web* (White 1974)   "Where's Papa going with that ax?" said Fern to her mother as they were setting the table for breakfast.

•❖*The Tale of Despereaux* (DiCamillo 2003)   This story begins within the walls of a castle, with the birth of a mouse.

•❖*The Chocolate Touch* (Catling 1995)   Most of the time John Midas was a very nice boy.

•❖*Love, Ruby Lavender* (Wiles 2001)   "Murderers! You can't have them all!" Ruby Lavender leaned out the car window and shook her fist.

•❖*Hoot* (Hiaasen 2002)   Roy would not have noticed the strange boy if it weren't for Dana Matherson, because Roy ordinarily didn't look out the window of the school bus.

Nonfiction

•❖From the *Atlanta Journal Constitution*, September 19, 2004, "Youngest Victim Mourned"   With water around his waist, one hand anchored to a tree branch and the other keeping his teenage daughter's head above the swelling drainage ditch, Rhys Terrill knew a precious link was missing from their tenuous human chain.

•❖*Harvesting Hope: The Story of Cesar Chavez* (Krull 2003)   Until Cesar Chavez was ten, every summer night was like a fiesta.

•❖*Understanding September 11th* (Frank 2002)   I can still remember the boom of the first explosion.

•❖*The Great Fire* (Murphy 1995)   The fire that swept through the heart of Chicago began on Sunday night, October 8, 1871. The Great Fire would burn for the rest of Sunday, all of Monday, and into the early hours of Tuesday with little real opposition.

•❖*Gleam and Glow* (Bunting 2001)   When Papa left to join the underground, Marina cried. To be truthful, Mama and I cried too.

•❖*Thank You, Sarah: The Woman Who Saved Thanksgiving* (Anderson 2002)   You think you know everything about Thanksgiving, don't you?

Once we have the leads on chart paper, we take a moment to talk about why these leads grab our attention as readers. Some are questions, while others sound mysterious. The beginning to *The Tale of Despereaux* is straightforward, almost plain, but it's mysterious too, because stories about castles (very huge) rarely start with a mouse (very tiny).

Some have fascinating facts, while others catch us off guard. The lead to the article "Youngest Victim Mourned" tugs at every heartstring as a picture of survival is clearly painted. All the leads cause the reader to wonder … to continue reading without skipping a beat.

This mini-lesson and work in the notebook engages students in two important aspects of revision. First, they are reading like writers. They are using other writers' work to inform them about good writing. Second, they are considering their own writing. In the reflection part of this lesson, students are asking themselves what they want to accomplish in their writing. What do they want the reader to infer from their leads?

I follow up this lesson a day or two later with a second mini-lesson that shows students how to revise their lead sentences. I start by asking them to go to the next blank page in the back of their notebooks, where we keep revision notes. They write "Try Ten" on the top of the page. This is a revision strategy. It will work for leads, transition sentences, verbs, endings, and so on. For this lesson, I use the strategy to revise a grabber lead.

"For the past couple of days, we have been studying how authors grab our attention with the first sentence. I want you to look at the draft you're currently working on and read your lead sentence to your partner."

I wait while students turn to one another to share their lead sentences from their drafts. "Ours are terrible," says Shannon as she focuses her attention back on me.

"How many of you found that your lead sentence is bland, blah … in a word, lame?" I try to be a bit silly to ease the anxiety of anyone who doesn't have a grabber lead. They're embarrassed until they look around and notice that just about everyone has a hand in the air. "Okay, it's official. We need to work on that first sentence. After all, we want people to read our work. It'd be a shame if no one read it after one sentence."

"In your notebook, I asked you to write Try Ten. When I write a sentence that I don't like, it's helpful to write it in as many different ways as possible," I share. "I'm going to show you how to do this. Is there anyone who has a truly horrible, terrible, no-good lead? Our class is going to work together to revise it" (Figure 4–3).

Figure 4–3   *Read to Write Strategy: Try Ten*

How: In the writer's notebook, date the page and write Try Ten as the heading. Ask students to write the lead sentence of their pieces ten different ways. Number one on the list is the lead they have on the draft. Then, for the next nine tries, students rewrite the lead, varying sentence structure, varying the beginning of the sentence, or trying different kinds of leads like a question or an action lead.

Why? Most of the time, students will not spend a lot of time on one sentence. Because this is the first sentence, it deserves more attention. Ten seems to be the magic number for revision in most cases. As students rewrite and reword their leads, they are forced to start thinking more creatively. At times, the new lead may change the direction of the piece, but if it's a grabber lead, kids will often want to rewrite the draft.

Extensions: Students can use the Try Ten strategy for just about anything because it's a way to focus on one aspect of a writing piece. Try-Ten ending sentences or Try-Ten similes, for example. Also, there isn't a rule that says it has to be ten. I just like that number, and it does seem to work for my students. You can adjust the number for younger children or children with disabilities.

When we revise a student lead on chart paper, I make a simple list. Number one is the original horrible, terrible, no-good lead. Then I take ideas from students to see how we can rewrite this sentence in a more interesting way.

This is easier said than done, especially when students go to work in pairs or on their own to revise their leads. Usually students can whip up three or four different ways to rewrite their leads, but when they start hitting numbers six, seven, and eight, things get a little tougher. This is actually good. Students must start thinking more creatively—outside the box if you will. When working with the class, I might intervene at this point to suggest a more creative lead. This is often just the nudge they need to get their creative juices going.

It's hard work, but frequently students come up with a wonderful grabber lead near the end of this revision strategy.

Try Ten—Davis

1. Toby Keith is my hero because he loves our country more than anybody.
2. Toby Keith fights for our country like President Bush and Dick Chaney put together.
3. Toby Keith would make a better president than John Kerry.
4. Watch out John Kerry, here comes Toby.
5. Toby Keith is the greatest hero because he doesn't let anyone mess with America.
6. I think people should like America as much as Toby Keith.
7. Toby Keith stands for our country like a bulldozer.

8. If you don't love America, Toby will make you think twice.

9. Toby Keith is my everyday hero because he stands for our country like a rock.

10. Go Toby!

(Please note: Davis' political views are not necessarily those of this author.)

This all takes place in their notebooks. The students then rewrite the lead they want on the draft paper. Davis chose number nine, "Toby Keith is my everyday hero because he stands for our country like a rock." Notice that Davis tries several different ways to say Toby Keith is a patriot. He even compares Keith to the president. This kind of play with words and revisions would not happen if it had to go directly into a draft. It does happen in the notebook.

Keeping this activity in the notebook has several advantages. First, students are using their notebooks to support their revisions. Second, students now have class notes and samples of how to revise a lead sentence. Third, students can refer back to the strategy when they want to "try ten."

The following strategies use books that I truly enjoy reading. You might choose to use the same books, or you may have other books in mind that you love. The strategies work with any well-written text ... even student writing. The key to successful lessons is to use texts you love and that you have already read to the children. It's important to savor stories for the pleasure they were meant to give readers. *Then,* as writers, reread them, or parts of them, and tear them apart to see just how the authors created them.

Mapping the Text

As I mentioned before, I share the book *John Henry* by Julius Lester with all of my students, every year. I know that fourth graders, in general, need help describing what is happening in their pieces. They just want to tell the story. Creating images in the readers' minds is hard for any novice writer. Most of the time children, and some adults, will rely on the overuse of adjectives. In reality, active verbs create stronger images.

Passive verbs such as *is, are, have,* and *become* are verbs that do not hold an image on their own account. Try it: envision the word *is.* You can't do it, can you? Now try to envision the word *pulverize.* You can see something smashed to smithereens, can't you? Verbs that create active images are known as active verbs.

Linking verbs such as *to be* do not create images without the help of other words, so they are passive. If you use verbs of that nature, you rely on adjectives to build images in your reader's mind. Overreliance on adjectives weakens writing. (And yes, this is a grammar lesson to enhance writing. This is one way to weave grammar seamlessly into the writing workshop.)

To help my students understand this, we study an excerpt from Julius Lester's *John Henry*. Students are given the passage and glue it in their writer's notebooks while I show it on the overhead projector. After the children glue the piece down, they gather around me to begin the lesson.

"Today, we are going to practice reading like a writer," I begin. "You all have a copy of my favorite page from the book *John Henry*. I am going to read it to you twice. The first time, I just want you to listen. Try to picture what is happening. The second time I read it, I want you to pay attention to how Lester created these images."

"How do we do that?" asks Nick.

"Good question. When you notice a word, phrase, or sentence that you think is well written or that sounds good when I read it, then I want you to circle it. Off to the side jot down your thoughts about it and what you think Lester was trying to do."

"What if we don't know what he's trying to do and we just like it?" Judy asks.

"Then take a guess. We're studying his writing, so we may have some questions. That's okay. This is called Mapping the Text—we're going to mark it so we can look at how the author did what he did in his writing. It's like we're making a map."

I still get some *if-you-say-so* looks, but pencils are ready and I begin reading:

> John Henry sang and he hammered and the air danced and the rainbow shimmered and the earth shook and rolled from the blows of the hammer. Finally it was quiet. Slowly the dust cleared.
>
> Folks could not believe their eyes. The boulder was gone. In its place was the prettiest and straightest road they had ever seen. Not only had John Henry pulverized the boulder into pebbles, he had finished building the road.
>
> In the distance where the new road connected to the main one, the road crew saw John Henry waving good-bye, a hammer on each shoulder, the rainbow draped around him like love.

After reading it twice, I give the students some time to finish their thoughts. Then I interrupt those still writing, "What did you notice?"

Hands fly upward as children have circled and underlined and jotted notes all over their pages.

"I like the word *pulverized*," begins Jason. "It's better than *broke* or even *smashed*."

I circle the word *pulverized* and make a note that it's a good word choice.

Next, Martha points out, "I liked the smiles he uses."

"The smiles?" I ask.

"Yes, like the last line, the rainbow draped around him like love," she explains.

I circle the last part of the last sentence and note next to it that it is a simile as I explain what similes are to the class.

The hands keep going up, and I keep mapping the text on the overhead. Students who didn't notice some of these things are allowed to mark their texts as well.

Finally, a student timidly raises his hand, "Ms. B? I'm not sure if this is right, but I noticed something about the way you read it."

"What?" I ask.

"Well, you read the first sentence really fast like you were running out of breath. Then the second two sentences you read slowly. You did the opposite with the second paragraph."

"Okay." I don't know what he is getting at, because this is the first time someone has pointed that out to me.

"I was wondering, did the way you read it have to do with the length of the sentences? The first sentence is really long with no commas and you read it fast. The next two sentences are short and you read them slow."

I haven't noticed this before, but he is absolutely right. "Yes, you're right. I did that and I do think it has to do with the length of the sentence. Varying your sentence lengths can add excitement and speed to the way people read your work."

This is a full mini-lesson within itself. I now direct the students to try using one of the techniques we talked about in their writing. They might try focusing on their word choice, using similes, or varying the length of their sentences. Students use the pages in their notebooks next to the excerpt and practice emulating. I think it's important for kids to have not only the author's text but their own attempts at the style as well. Here's an example of a notebook entry that varies sentence length to breathe excitement into an otherwise mundane task:

> *The bell rang and students flood the halls filling it with laughter and shouts of joy and lockers slam and toilets flush while kids rush on to the next class. Classroom doors slam shut. Silence sweeps up the last bit of chatter. The next bell rings. The hallways are empty.*

The next day, we go back to this piece, because we still haven't talked about the verbs. I begin by showing them the text on the overhead again.

"There are about a hundred words here. How many do you think are adjectives?"

The answers range from twenty-five to fifty. A student caps the guesses off with, "Everyone knows you need a lot of adjectives to write a descriptive scene like that, Ms. B."

"That's absolutely wrong," I reply. Their mouths fall open—I have their attention.

"Only about 10 percent of these words are actually adjectives. That's a very small amount. How do you think Julius Lester created so many images in our head without using a ton of adjectives?"

Students begin talking to each other, somewhat taken aback by my conjecture that adjectives are not the primary image makers.

"Let's go back and make a list of the words we love in this piece. We'll put them into three lists—adjectives, nouns, and verbs." Students open their notebooks and begin creating the list for their own use. Our list looks something like this:

Adjectives	Nouns	Verbs
quiet	rainbow	sang
prettiest	earth	hammered
straightest	blows	danced
new	boulder	shimmered
	pebbles	shook
	love	rolled
		pulverized
		connected
		draped

Looking at the list, my students understand what I mean. The words that impressed us most are verbs, then nouns, then adjectives. The verbs are not just any kind of verbs; they are powerful image creators—powerful verbs are active verbs. This list that we created goes into our writer's notebooks. I choose to put it in the back section with other grammar lessons, because eventually this will lead us to a deeper study of active and passive voice. It's also a good word-sorting exercise that can be done again as a strategy when learning about other parts of speech.

This strategy is a surefire winner when it comes to mini-lessons and reading like a writer. It clarifies for children how to look at words in a different way. It establishes the importance of knowing the difference between nouns, verbs, and adjectives. The purpose is set for revising word choice. And students begin to understand the difference between passive and active voice in writing, even if I haven't given those labels yet. This lesson changes the way my students read like writers and the way they write (Figure 4–4).

Figure 4–4   *Read to Write Strategy: Mapping the Text*

How: Use an excerpt from a story the children have already read. Give them each a copy for their notebooks. Read the excerpt aloud twice. The first time the students listen, the second time they can begin to write on the excerpt. They circle words they like or phrases that grab them. Whatever they notice about the writing, they make a mark nearby somehow.

Why? This exercise gives students practice in the craft of reading like a writer. It allows students to take a step back and look at how the images and mood of the passage were put together.

Extensions: Have students play with some of the words and techniques they discover in their own writing—first in the notebook and eventually on drafts.

Poetry Pass

Reading excerpts from picture books and novels with students is a great way to help them start reading like writers. There is a lot to learn from the largely untapped resource of poetry, too. No wonder our kids don't like poetry—they're not exposed to it nearly enough. It's the part in the anthology some teachers will skip.

The best reason to use poetry in the classroom is that poems are short. This is an important selling point, especially for struggling readers and writers. Poems are easy to read and easy to write. They frequently focus on one image or feeling, and use as few words as possible to get the meaning across. What more could a struggling student want? When it comes to poetry, less is often more.

When students try to rhyme, they tend to focus more on getting the rhyme right than on creating the image. Luckily, there is a lot of poetry out there that doesn't rhyme. I often avoid rhyming poetry in my classroom simply to help expose children to other ways to write it. I cannot tell you the number of times students have totally turned on to poetry once I have lifted the burden of having to rhyme.

I have seen Lee Bennett Hopkins, an icon in children's poetry, and read his work at various conferences. He rhymes, and the anthologies he creates contain rhyming poetry. I went to talk to him after one of his readings and explained to him that my students want to rhyme but often end up writing shallow poems because they're more focused on the rhyme than anything else. I admitted to him that I finally told my students they were not allowed to rhyme during their first attempts at poetry. I also admitted to using mostly nonrhyming poetry as models in my classroom, then asked how I could do a better job teaching rhyme so my students could write it well. His response has stayed with me.

He told me he once taught sixth grade, and he too encouraged the kids to write nonrhyming poetry. He explained to me that the rhyme should come naturally and enhance the poem, not take away from it. But he also said that if children never read rhyming poetry they'll never understand how to use it well.

I have anthologies of poetry in my classroom, some with rhyming poetry and some without. If a child is a natural at rhyming, I encourage it. If a child is forcing the rhyme, I do one of two things. I encourage the child to read poetry that rhymes and "study" how it works, makes sense, and enhances the poetry. Or I discourage the writer from using rhyme at this time. Writing should sound natural, not forced.

There is also a lot that children can learn from poets to enhance their prose writing. A good friend of mine who teaches Advance Placement English classes at the local high school once said to me, "If you don't know poetry, you'll never write well." I think there is a lot of truth to that. Poetry focuses on images and uses different ways to create those images. From similies and metaphors to word choice and form, there is no law that says you can't use these same techniques in prose writing. So we often read poetry as writers in an effort to help children make that genre connection.

The Poetry Pass has been a helpful activity in my classroom. It's an activity, not a strategy. It takes most of the class period each time we do it. However, it's a class period full of reading and studying writing. The conversations are rich and the ideas for writing flow. It's well worth the class time.

I start by having students read and discuss poetry. In order to do this activity well, I have the students read and discuss poetry during our reading workshop for a few weeks ahead of time. Reading and discussing poetry as readers is an important first step. We then go back and look through the writing aspect.

I love working with e. e. cummings' work—if for no other reason than how easy it is to notice things about his writing. Any poet(s) will work, however. Use the ones you love.

I choose three or four poems for this activity; I retype them on a sheet of legal-sized paper because I want all of the poems on the same page and room for the students to write around the poems as well. Essentially, students are going to map the text—like they did for *John Henry*—but there is a twist.

I begin by reading the poems aloud—twice. Then the students have five minutes to map the text. At the end of the five minutes they put their names on the papers and pass them to someone else in the room. For the next minute, students silently reread the poems and the comments that the previous students wrote. Then I give them another three minutes to mark the text, adding their comments. Again, we pass the papers to someone else in the room.

This time I give the students two minutes to reread the poems and comments on the page in front of them, then another three minutes to write on the text. This time, students can mark things they have been noticing and things they noticed other students noticing. After the time is up for this round, the papers go back to the first students who had them.

Now, students are looking at a page full of poetry, their comments, and the comments of two or three other students. We take time to read the papers silently. I then give the students five minutes or so to discuss this in small groups. What did they notice? What did they learn from other students? What questions do they still have?

After five minutes, the class gathers with their papers in the front of the room, where I have the same poems on a transparency. We discuss the poems and the writing. During the discussion, students continue to jot down things other students noticed but they did not. By the time we're finished, students have a good idea of some of the techniques e. e. cummings uses—repetition, syllable rhythms, metaphors, and images—throughout his poetry.

At the end of the activity, students choose from the sheet of poems we have been working with the one that they learned the most from. The students then cut-and-paste this into the writer's notebook and write a reflection on the day's activity. When we go back to the writing workshop format the next day, students are asked to try some of these techniques in their writing (Figure 4–5).

Here are two student poems inspired by e. e. cummings.

Ryan (Inspired by "little tree"—one capital letter)
"i wish"
i wish
i had a million dollars
but
i don't
i wish i had a big screen tv in my room
but
i don't
i wish
i didn't have to go to school
but
I do

Marissa (Inspired by "&sun&"—broken words)
"snowflakes"
snowflakes
e
very
one
is
not
the
s
am
e
f
a
ll
ing
d
o
w
n
to
th
e
ground

Figure 4–5   *Read to Write Strategy: Poetry Pass*

How: Find four poems of a poet you love. Retype them on one page of legal-size paper, leaving plenty of room between and around the poems. Give each child a copy of the poetry. Read through the poems twice—the first time for listening and the second time to begin mapping the poems. After a few minutes, have each pass his or her paper to someone else. Kids take a moment to read the comments already on the page, and then they begin to mark the poems again. After a few minutes, they pass again, and repeat the process.

Why? Using poetry is a quick and manageable way to invite children to look at a writer's craft. Many of the same techniques used in poetry can be used in prose—specific word choice, rhythm, repetition, metaphors, etc.

Extensions: Students cut out a poem from the poetry pass sheet from which they learned a lot about writing. They glue it into their notebooks and reflect on their learning that day. Students try to emulate the style in their own poetry or prose. This can be done again and again with different poets, styles of poetry, and even short excerpts of prose or nonfiction.

Author Style

As I have studied other writers, I have noticed style similarities between Julius Lester, e. e. cummings, and Cynthia Rylant; specifically, the way they use similes and metaphors. Their writing is powerful in its simplicity. I love Cummings' simile from the poem "maggie and millie and molly and may": "as small as a world and as large as alone." Lester uses a simile in his book, *John Henry,* "a mountain as hard as hurt feelings." Notice how similar these are in style—the use of opposite images to create a new one. The world is a large, large place and yet it is described as small. Who would have thought of alone being large, when you're alone you're single, by yourself, small. And when my feelings are hurt, I feel sad, vulnerable while a mountain seems strong and powerful. Yet, the images provoked in my mind make perfect sense. I know exactly what those feelings are like, and I can try to emulate this in my own writing. By studying the styles of different writers and making connections between them, we create a web of mentors from which to learn.

As students begin to study authors, I have them keep a chart in the back of their notebooks to record their findings. Sometimes when they're stuck in their writing, they need to reread a model of the style they're trying to emulate. Having the chart handy in the notebook helps them reference whenever and wherever they're writing. In creating this chart as a class, we make an anchor chart, working with the authors our whole class is studying. Students then go to their own reading and find their own writing mentors to put on their own charts in their notebooks (Figure 4–6).

Figure 4-6 *Author Style Chart*

Author	Style	Example	Text Reference
e. e. cummings	similes that are oxymorons	"as small as a world and as large as alone."	poem: "maggie and milly and molly and may"
Julius Lester	strong verbs	"he pulverized the boulder into pebbles"	*John Henry*
Ralph Fletcher	writing small	"Silence. For a full five seconds, nobody moved."	*Fig Pudding*
Elizabeth Friedrich	repetition	"Again no one moved. No one said a word. No one even seemed to breathe."	*Leah's Pony*
Andrew Clements	characterization writing small	"But Mrs. Granger seemed like a giant. It was her eyes that did it."	*Frindle*
Kate Klise	play on words— humor, hidden connections	Rhett Tyle Anna Conda (sleezy antagonists' names) Lilly Watson (protagonist) S. Holmes (Lilly's teacher)	*Trial by Journal*
Kathleen Krull	plain— straightforward writing that rips your heart out	"a teacher hung a sign on him that read, I AM A CLOWN. I SPEAK SPANISH. He came to hate school"	*Harvesting Hope: The Story of Cesar Chavez*
Russell Freedman	grabber leads in biographies	action lead: "Painted and dressed for battle and singing war songs, the warriors formed orderly columns and rode out of their great encampment on the Powder River."	"Red Cloud" from *Indian Chiefs*

This chart can be used in a variety of ways. Students might keep a list of different authors and the elements of their style or concentrate on one author's work. It's important for kids to include a short example and the title of the reference text on the chart. Students may not give the proper literary name for the style, and the example helps to show what they want to emulate. The text reference column allows children and teachers to refer to the inspirational writing in its full-text format.

There are times that students want to do independent author studies. They may then keep a chart on just one author. Or they may want to study how three authors use a similar style or approach to writing and keep that on one chart. Or the chart can be used to list the different elements of style noticed in a particular text by a particular author (Figure 4–7).

Figure 4–7   *Read to Write Strategy: Charting Authors' Styles*

How: Using chart paper, create a chart like the one provided in the appendix. Give students copies of a blank chart to put in their notebooks or have them create one on a blank page in the back of their notebooks. Using authors you have studied, show students how to begin filling out the chart as a record of different author styles.

Why? This requires students to synthesize what they're learning about authors' styles. It also creates a reference tool for children when they want to write like Gary Paulsen, for instance. They will have an example of what that means—what Paulsen does and how he does it.

Extension: Students continue to work on their own individual charts with their own writing mentors.

When our class is reading like writers for a sense of style and craft, it takes a lot of pressure off me to know everything there is to know about writing. Rather, I learn along with them, I marvel at what authors are doing and am not afraid to say, "I hadn't noticed that before … let's try it in our notebooks." Learning how to take advantage of all the authors sitting on the bookshelves in my classroom has been the best thing I've done for myself—as a writer and as a teacher.

It's an overwhelming task, especially if you have a large classroom library. But, if you noticed how I wrote this chapter, I mentioned a couple of authors whose work I know well. I used the example of *John Henry* repeatedly. Start small, know one or two books well, and teach from them all year. Then, as your students do the same, they'll teach you about other books. And soon, you'll have a collection of books you know well enough to read … like a writer.

Chapter 5:

❧

Using Notebooks to Understand Genre

When I bought my current home, I bought it brand-new. I looked through the model homes and found the one I liked. I noticed how the kitchen was laid out, where the bedrooms were, and whether there was room for all of my child's toys. I looked at the "craft" of the house. I signed over my savings, and the builders went to work.

I visited my homesite occasionally to check on the progress. I couldn't tell the kitchen from the dining room and, looking at it, didn't see how they were going to fit all the features I saw in the models. I worried, but the builder kept saying this was just the framework to hold my house up. The insides would look like the model when it was done.

As writers, we need to understand how to build a strong structural foundation for our writing before we decorate it. This structure, in literary terms, is known as genre. Understanding the elements of different genres enables writers to develop their writing appropriately. Similarly knowing the different writing choices they have allows children a wider range of possibilities. It's not enough to say, "These are the qualities of fantasy," or "To write an essay you must do this and that." Student writers (and this includes adults) need to read and write a lot in order to understand the dynamics of a genre and how it affects the reader. This knowledge is vital as writers go to write—after all, someone is going to read it.

The strategies in this chapter are applied during the revision stages of the writing process. Students will likely already have a draft. In my class, drafts are done on yellow legal pads. It helps us keep the draft separate from the final copies. I have found that students are more interested in working on revisions if they know they're not going to have to write things over and over again. So the strategies presented here are all done in the notebook. That way students have a record of the strategy to revisit as needed. They can also try the strategy in the notebook to have an example. Then if they choose to use the revision, they can add it to the piece. If not, the draft is still intact.

Understanding Genre Structure

Genre structure is important for readers as well as writers because readers depend on the structures to help them predict and create the framework for the story within their minds. If readers are expecting fantasy, they're looking for good versus evil and wondering, Who is the hero? What is his quest? If the reader has chosen realistic fiction, however, she or he is expecting to identify with the main character in an emotional or intellectual way. The plot of the story needs to be plausible and the solution attained reasonably. These things make a difference to a reader.

I often engage my students in genre studies not only in the reading workshop but also in the writing workshop. Working from the back of the notebook, we draw a chart to record our findings and to use as a reference later. I rely on three-column charts for this. As we look at the elements of different genres, I ask the students to think about how the elements affect them as readers and how they affect them as writers.

Nonfiction		
What I can expect as a reader …	Elements of nonfiction writing	What I need to know as a writer …

When we work on a genre chart like this, it doesn't matter if it's during reading workshop time or writing workshop time. We're talking about both reading and writing. Since fourth graders are generally not used to connecting their reading to writing, I have students put this chart in their writer's notebooks. Keeping this chart in the writer's notebook reinforces the reading and writing connection.

In the back of the notebook, I have the students create a three-column chart. They then write the same headings on the chart as I have on mine. "Elements of …" in the middle column, "What I can expect as a reader …" in the left column, and "What I need to know as a writer …" in the right column.

I might start the lesson by saying, "We've been reading a lot of nonfiction in our reading workshop lately. Let's take some time to write down what we have learned about nonfiction text and how it helps us as readers."

This seems harmless enough and several children raise their hands. "The title of the article or book is important," begins Joey.

I write "Title" in the middle column. "Why is it important for the reader, Joey?"

"Because it tells you what it's going to be about. We can start to ask questions on the title."

I write under the left-hand, or reader, column: The reader knows the topic of the text and can begin to ask questions.

"Sometimes there is a subtitle, Ms. B," Shannon adds.

In the middle column, under "Title," I write "Subtitle." "Okay, Shannon, what is helpful about a subtitle?"

"It gives you more information about the piece in case the title is misleading or not clear."

"You're right, the subtitle gives us more information or clarifies the title." In the reader column, I write: This helps clarify the topic for the reader. Reader can again ask predicting questions based on the subtitle.

"Okay," I pause from the chart, "let's stop here for a moment. Let's think about why it's important for writers to know what readers expect from the title."

Blank stares.

I try again. "When we go to write a nonfiction piece, why is it helpful for us to know that readers want the title to reflect the topic?"

A couple of brave souls raise their hands.

"If you know readers are going to expect something about the topic in the title, then you know how to write your title," says Joey.

"Right. In nonfiction, readers are looking for information on a topic, so the title should reflect that. Let's write that in the writer column next to the word 'Title.'"

"What about the subtitle?" I ask, "Why is it important for writers to use subtitles?"

More hands go up. "If the writer uses a catchy title or a title that doesn't exactly give the topic, then she can use a subtitle to tell the reader more about the topic," reports Marissa.

"You got it," I respond. We add this to the chart under the writer column.

Although this may seem like a trivial exercise, ten-year-olds do not think this way. They do not naturally think about what they know as readers to help them write for an audience of readers. It just doesn't occur to them. So as we continue to make this chart, little lightbulbs start going off as the connection finally comes through (Figures 5–1, 5–2).

Figure 5–1 *Nonfiction Feature Anchor Chart*

What I can expect as a reader ...	Nonfiction features	How this helps me as a writer ...
The title will give you an idea of what the book or article is about. Think about what you know about the subject of the title to predict what the book will tell you.	Title	Your title should catch the reader's eye. It should give the reader a clue to what your writing is about. It's your first hook to reel the reader in.
Scan the table of contents found at the beginning of the book. This gives you an idea of the topics that will be covered. If you're looking for a specific topic, you can go directly to that page. This also sets the framework for you as you read.	Table of contents	This is the organization of your book. It's like an outline of what topics will be covered. It should be in a logical order and use headings that grab the reader's attention. It should also give the reader cues as to what the book will be about and how it is structured.
These are within each section of the book and are usually in bold print. They indicate a change in topic. If you take the subheading and change it into a question, you set your purpose for reading—to answer the question.	Subheadings	The use of subheadings helps you guide the reader as you change ideas within a topic. It should be written clearly enough that if the reader changed the subheading into a question, the question would be answered in the following text.
Important words are usually put in bold or italic print. Pay attention to these words. Often the meaning is in the context of the story or is at the bottom of the page, called a footnote.	Bold print or italics	Use bold print or italics to catch your reader's attention. It's saying, HEY THIS IS AN IMPORTANT WORD TO KNOW. Then be sure to give the meaning of the word, either in the text or at the bottom of the page in a footnote.
Don't skip these. Pictures and diagrams are important in nonfiction. They give you extra tidbits of information that help you understand the whole story.	Pictures and diagrams	Provide pictures, photos, diagrams, maps, graphs, etc., to help the reader visualize what you are writing about. Remember, a picture is worth a thousand words.
Beneath pictures and diagrams are usually captions. Captions tell you more about the picture. They help you understand why the author put it in there. Take care to read these carefully.	Captions	Beneath any pictures or diagrams you insert into your story, you need a caption. This is a brief statement or two helping the reader understand the picture and link it back to the story.

Figure 5–2 *Fable Anchor Chart*

How this helps me as a reader …	Elements of fables	How this helps me as a writer …
The animals have humanlike thoughts and relationships. This helps me identify with them.	Characters— usually animals	The animals you use should have an obvious relationship—like pigs and wolves. They are characterized like people, not real animals.
There is a problem that must be solved. The main character will work to solve the problem.	Problem of the story	There must be something the main character wants but has a problem getting. A solution must be attainable.
The problem is solved by the end of the story. Usually there is a lesson to be learned from the solution.	Solution	The solution must be reasonable. Often there is a lesson you are trying to teach the reader.
This is the lesson of the story. What is the writer trying to tell me?	Moral	There needs to be a life lesson you're trying to teach. It must be evident in the solution.

The charts that we create hang in our classroom and are situated neatly in the back of each writer's notebook. They become a useful tool for students during their revisions as well as for me for when I confer with them. The charts are a reference to help my students be aware of the reader's needs as they write. Likewise, this strategy for the reading-writing connection helps them as readers. The students begin to expect things from the authors of their books and articles. They use this information to structure their own understanding and read with a more critical eye (Figure 5–3).

Figure 5–3 *Genre Strategy: Text Elements*

How: Using a three-column chart, list the elements of the genre you are studying. Then in the left-hand column, have students think about how each element helps them as readers. In the right-hand column, students turn their thinking to why they need to know about each element as writers.

Why? This strategy helps students focus on the importance of structure within their writing. Too often, kids just write without giving much thought to their audience, the reader. This chart helps students focus on the reader's needs and how to fulfill them as writers.

Extension: Use existing charts in the revision phases. Does the piece have the appropriate elements? If not, fix it. This can also be used in reading workshop, during guided reading, or during literature circles to help guide conversations around the elements in the text students can use to support their comprehension.

Playing with Features

Once students understand the elements of the genre we're working with, they're able to write more purposefully. But they'll still need to revise and go back to their notebooks to play with the genre features. I say "play" because revision, while difficult, should be playful. Sometimes our best thinking comes when we're playing around with words. We're more relaxed and more willing to try things. So we play.

"Today you'll need your notebooks for some fun," I begin. "Today we're going to play with some of the features of nonfiction in our notebooks."

"What do you mean *play*?" Shannon asks cautiously. She likes to know what to do and how to do it right. "I thought writing was work and we're working on a draft."

"Well, sometimes even writers want to have some fun. Of course, writing fun is a little bit of work."

"I knew it!" shouts Matthew. "Nothing is as it seems with you, Ms. B." He casts a quick grin to let us all know he was in the "play" mode.

"Be that as it may, today we're going to play with headings. In your articles you have all written headings when you change ideas. I want you to look at your draft then, in your notebook, make a list of your headings."

The students begin writing down the headings from their drafts in a list. This will isolate phrases so we can look at them out of context and see the headings as a group.

"Now, reread your headings, and jot down any thoughts you have or anything you notice about them."

A few people make notes, and some just stare at their notebooks. I put them out of their agony, as it's obvious some of them haven't seen the fun in this ... yet.

"What did you notice?" I ask.

"Mine are boring," says Matthew. "I mean they're not boring in my article, but when I look at them this way they just look ... blah."

"My headings all start the same way," adds Marissa, "I guess that's not good. I mean if we don't want all of our sentences starting the same way, do we want our headings to do that?"

Other students start rereading their lists to see what they notice. Joey blurts out in excitement, "I have a cool subheading." His voice drains of excitement as he continues, "Only one, though. The rest are kind of blah."

"Okay, you see you have some work to do, but I want you to have some fun with these headings first."

"Fun with headings?" the kids give me quizzical looks.

"Try rearranging the words in your subheadings. Is there another way to say the same thing that has a bit more oomph to it? Try creating headings that, when you put them together, have a message for the reader."

"Oh, like a secret code," smiles Matthew.

"I don't know, maybe. I just think we can be more creative in using the headings. So play today. Be creative and have fun. It doesn't mean this has to go into your draft … we're just seeing what happens."

Off they go, some in pairs and some alone, to play with writing. We get some silly ideas and some darn good ones. This allows the kids to see the fun of revision—of rethinking an old thing in a new way. One student comes up with these headings for his persuasive piece about ten-year-olds needing cell phones:

Draft Headings	Playful Headings
Age Shouldn't Matter	**A**ge Discrimination No More!
Know Where Your Child Is	**B**eing There
I Can Talk to My Friends	**C**ommunication Is Key

Notice the way the headings changed. This child thought it would be fun to have the ABCs in his heading. So he went back to try to arrange them—rewrite them—in such a way that each heading started with the next letter of the alphabet.

As children play with text features, they'll sometimes get very creative and sometimes not. That's the point, though—to play and see what happens (Figure 5–4).

Figure 5–4 *Genre Strategy: Playing with Features*

How: In the mini-lesson, review one feature of the genre your class is writing. Ask students to reread this feature (like headings) throughout their pieces. Then break students up into pairs to *play* with the features, making them more interesting or creative.

Why? I often find that during a genre study, when we all are working within the same genre, students tend to become too focused on the elements they need in the piece. Their writing becomes dry and dull as they spend their energy on getting the structure correct. This strategy breathes some life into their work, as it helps them to remember writing can be fun.

Extension: Use this quick strategy with any rereading of written work. The key is to let students know they're playing with words—they should loosen up a bit and have fun. Often the creativity released is amazing.

Genre Switch

For seven years, I tried to write a poem that captured a particular moment in my childhood—which I can see vividly in my mind. I'm eight or nine years old, growing up in a suburb of Chicago. It's probably early evening in the winter, but it's dark like the middle of the night. I remember being bundled up and playing in the snow as my dad shoveled the driveway. Looking up in the sky, I see it has started to snow again. I remember standing there, in the middle of my front yard, just looking up into those thousands of snowflakes falling down. I remember feeling as if I were caught inside one of those snow shakers you can buy around the holidays. Inside the clear plastic ball there is a scene of some sort with water or mountains, and when you shake it, it snows . . . and snows and snows.

As an adult, I was convinced this was the making of a poem. I tried writing it—over and over. Nine of my notebooks have musings of this poem as I tried to force this memory, this moment, into a genre where it did not want to go. Finally, during a summer writing institute I was attending, I decided to try writing about it as a metaphor—which led me to a story. After years of trying, I finally wrote about this moment, not as the poem I first thought it would be, but rather as a short story.

Children don't envision how they'll write. Most of them assume that their writing will fit neatly into a story or narrative format. In a writing workshop setting, students have choices, which at times means choosing the genre that best fits the topic. One way I can help children note different ways to write about a topic is with an exercise called Genre Switch.

"Open to the next blank page in your notebook," I begin. "Today you're going to write about the topic of a piece you're working on, but in a different way. In your notebook, I want you to start writing. Every few minutes, I'm going to name a new genre. You are to begin writing about your topic in that genre until we switch again. Sometimes the genre will seem difficult to write in, and sometimes it will be really easy. Stick with it."

The kids are looking at me as if I've finally gone off the deep end, but they know better than to try to change my mind when it comes to writing. So they dutifully open their notebooks, ready to begin.

"Begin writing realistic fiction." And we write. Whatever each child's topic is, he or she is writing as if it's a realistic fiction piece. After a few minutes I say, "Fairy tale." No matter where they are in their stories, students switch their writing style to sound like a fairy tale. "Now try spooky story." I continue with newspaper article, poem, fantasy, and encyclopedia.

It looks something like this:

> Three days after my fourth birthday my dad came home extremely upset. He had taken my dog Chelsea to the vet. She had heart problems.
>
> EXTRA EXTRA READ ALL ABOUT IT! Chelsea's Heart Breaks at Vet Office! The vet refuses to comment as the saddened father of two goes home to tell his children the news.
>
> As the little girl cried, her fairy godmother appeared from her tears. "Whatever is the matter, honey?" "My doggie died," she said. she cried and cried. "If you wipe those tears away, I'll grant you a wish."
>
> Tears stopped
> wishes came to mind
> for Chelsea
> dear Chelsea
> to be alive
> POOF
> She LIVES
> she lives
> in my heart
> not
> deep down
> but
> up front

When we're finished I ask, "When did you have the most energy to write? Which genre seemed the easiest to you for your topic?"

Children were sometimes amazed to know it wasn't the reliable realistic fiction. Some found an article format was easy, others poetry. It became instantly clear to them, however, that sometimes our topics need to choose the genre and, as writers, we need to be open to the different possibilities of the piece (Figure 5–5).

Figure 5–5   Genre Strategy: Genre Switch

How: Students write about self-selected topics in their notebooks. Every minute or two I call out a different genre. Students continue writing but switch their style to match the genre I called out. I do this as few as four times and as many as eight within one sitting.

Why? It's a great way to explore different genres in your writing without having to write an entire entry in different genres. Also, it opens children up to the possibilities of genres for their topics.

Extension: Students can use this technique on their own or even with each other in peer conferences.

Understanding the Structure of Story to Write Well

When children read and can retell a story, it is easy to think they know what makes a good story. But many children don't. They don't stop to think, how does this story follow plot structure or how do I use plot structure to write better stories? Understanding story structure helps young writers to focus their stories and develop their ideas. My favorite question to ask the children at the beginning of the year is: When you write, what makes a good story? The answers from the students are the same year after year. "It is something I know." "It has a problem." "It's long." "I use correct spelling." And sure enough, someone launches into a discussion of the novel they're writing at home.

"I'm on Chapter 8 and I haven't even gotten to the good part yet!" Holy cow! If he's on Chapter 8 without a good part, what the heck is he writing? I'd hate to be the editor of *that* piece of work.

My second favorite question to ask is: How many of you have ever written a grocery-list story?

"Huh?" is the resounding response. "What's that?"

"A grocery-list story is a story that just goes on and on. For example: I went to Six Flags. I got up early. We had breakfast. My mom told us to get dressed for Six Flags. We were excited. The car ride there was long. We got stuck in traffic. We had to park far away. And so on . . . ."

A few hands begin to go up. "Come on," I say, "Confess. You have all done it, haven't you?"

Smiles and giggles of familiarity with this story leak out of the students.

These two questions help students see exactly where they are developmentally in their writing. Most nine- and ten-year-olds either write long, unending stories that never establish a plot or they write a list of events, one after the other.

I am lucky enough to work in a school where writer's workshop is the norm in all grades. I have kids who understand the writing process and use the writing notebook at the beginning of the year. Despite this, students may still come to me writing lists or plotless stories, which is why I think this is a developmental place in their writing journey in which kids get stuck. This is also about the time many teachers move into report writing and writing across the curriculum, and the students don't ever really move beyond this kind of narrative writing.

It's important that children know how to write narratives to hone their reading and writing skills. Understanding how to put a good narrative story together also gives children the practice and background they will need to progress to more demanding kinds of writing.

The following three strategies help students develop plot in their writing. By studying reading like writers, students begin to understand the importance of plot structure as readers and writers.

Understanding Plot Structure

Knowing plot structure is essential to writing a story. We study this in reading for comprehension reasons. It's helpful for readers to expect certain elements in the story. Readers look for main characters, the setting, a problem, a resolution, and a wrap-up to the story. We teach our children to understand this structure as readers, but in writing, we often focus solely on beginning, middle, and end. It stands to reason that a student's idea of beginning, middle, and end may look like a grocery list:

My Day At Six Flags:
Beginning of the day: I woke up and we got ready.
Middle of the day: We rode rides and ate lunch.
End of the day: We finally went home. I fell asleep in the car.

Once students understand story structure, not only as readers but as writers, they have a better understanding of why "My Day at Six Flags" is a difficult topic to write about.

I go back to using a comparative chart like I use for genre studies. Students make an anchor chart in their notebooks to compare story structure for readers and writers. We begin by discussing what we have studied about plot as readers, then look at how this knowledge helps us as writers when writing a story. It ends up looking something like the chart in Figure 5–6.

Figure 5–6 *Anchor Chart for Plot*

How this helps us as readers …	Story plot structure	How this helps us as writers …
Expect to meet the main character (protagonist), find out the setting, and what the character wants.	Beginning (Who? Wants What?)	Introduce the main character (protagonist), establish the setting, and determine what the character wants.
Every story has a problem. Something gets in the way of what the protagonist wants—an antagonist (character) usually is part of the problem.	Conflict/problem (But?)	Every story *has* to have a problem that can and will be solved. Writers often use an antagonist character to perpetuate the problem and get in the way of a solution.
Things that happen in the story show the character struggling with the problem.	Rising action (So?)	Create events in your story that show the protagonist trying to solve the problem.
Problems in stories will be solved. Look for the event that is the key to solving the problem.	Climax—event leading to problem solution (So?)	This is an event or happening in your story that lets the reader know the problem will be (or is) solved.
After the climax, you know the problem is solved. This part of the story is what happens because the problem is solved. It leads to the ending.	Falling action—the things that happen because the problem is solved. (Then?)	After the climax, the problem is solved. So what happens since the problem is out of the way??? Give the character what she or he wants.
The ending wraps up the story for the reader. It gives you a sense of completeness.	Ending—wrapping up the story by satisfying the reader that the problem is solved and the character gets what he or she wants.	The ending should give the reader a sense of completeness. Everything is going to be okay. It's the part where you wrap up the story.

The conversation in creating this chart is useful as students begin to see what they have not been doing in their writing. This is the clearest way I have found to move students from the grocery list to a true story. As students write their drafts and revise, they have this page in their notebooks open and refer to it. It becomes a useful guide for students and a talking point during conferring.

Story Summaries

There is plenty of research that consistently mentions summarizing as an essential skill for learning. In *Classroom Instruction that Works: Research Based Strategies for Increasing Student Achievement*, the authors refer to summarizing as one of the "most powerful skills students can cultivate" (Marzano et al. 2001, p. 48). Max Thompson, most well-known for his Focused Learning Schools, makes an explicit point to teachers that students need to summarize their learning after each lesson. Summarizing is one of the most efficient and effective ways to help students absorb what they're learning. Being able to take what one knows and synthesize it into a summary is a higher-level thinking skill.

Summarizing is a skill we have been using as readers for years. When my students begin writing in their reading notebooks about the book they're reading, the first thing they do is summarize what they have read. This lets me know where they are in the book and whether they are truly comprehending what they are reading. If the summary is vague, their comprehension is likely vague as well.

Likewise, summarizing is essential in writing. Students should have a concise idea of what they're writing. They should have a sense of the problem, solution, and ending. This helps writers stay focused in their work. So as I teach this reading skill, I flip it into a writer's tool for revision.

The best way I have learned to help children synthesize information and summarize just about anything is by asking these simple questions:

Who? (Who is the character?)
Wants What? (What does the character want in the story?)
But? (What is the problem? What gets in the way of the character getting what she or he wants?)
So? (So, what does the character do to solve the problem?)
Then? (And then what happens? What's the wrap-up? How does the reader know the character moves on?)

The responses to these questions fit into a nice, tight paragraph. I often open my reading workshop with a summary of what we read the day before, to help the kids get back into the story. It also helps students distinguish the important details from the entertaining details. As my class worked with this strategy in reading, I realized this could help us as writers and decided to try it.

I gather the children around the easel, which has a chart with these questions: Who? Wants What? But? So? Then?

"Hey," Joey says excitedly as he sits down with his writer's notebook, "I thought we were going to write. I'm almost finished with a story I'm writing."

"Joey, you'll have time to write, I promise," I reply. "I was thinking about all the work we have been doing with summarization in reading. It occurred to me that this skill might help us with our writing as well."

"How?" asks Joey, trying to move the conversation along so he can get to his own writing agenda.

"When you go to write today and work on your drafts, I want you to start by rereading what you've written." I pause. "Then I want you to try to summarize your own writing, much like we have been summarizing the books you've been reading."

"By using those questions?" asks Marissa.

"Yes. In your notebook, try to write a summary of your story. Make sure, though, you base your summary on what you have actually written, not what you have meant to write. Take a moment to do that now."

The students begin rereading their drafts. Slowly, I see them move from reading to responding in their notebooks. Some students do this easily, some get stuck.

"How is it going?" I ask after a few minutes have passed.

"I got the Who? Wants what? questions. I don't think I have a problem though," responds Joey.

"I don't have a problem either. Actually, my character doesn't seem to want anything. What happens if we can't answer these questions, Ms. B.?" asks Shannon.

"Good question. What do you think?" My students have been writing with me long enough to think through this together.

"Then we have to go back and revise," says Joey. "A reader should be able to summarize any story he reads." So he *has* been paying attention during reading.

"You're right. If you can't summarize your own story, neither can your reader. Knowing which questions you can't answer will help you go back and revise your story."

Students' heads nod, and some begin noting the questions they can't answer.

"Before you go to revise and work today, I want you to write in your notebook questions you can't answer about your story. Then make a quick plan in your notebook about what you need to do. That way, you won't forget as you get back to writing." Students will put this work in the back of the notebook where we keep revision, editing, and grammar strategies. The date at the top of the entry and a quick title will help students locate this entry later.

Writing a plan of what they need to do is an important step. Usually, kids want to go from noting what they need to do directly to writing. Some kids can do this, but many will end up forgetting what they wanted to write to answer those questions. Taking some time to think through the revisions and make some notes is helpful. I find this helpful in my own writing. It's easy to get wrapped up in a story and forget what you wanted to do in the first place. This is what leads to those long, never-ending stories—a habit I try to break (Figure 5–7).

Figure 5–7 *Genre Strategy: Summarizing Your Story*

How: When students write a narrative or piece of fiction, the reader should be able to summarize the story. Students ask themselves the following questions about their work: Who? Wants what? But? So? Then? The questions they can't answer, based on the stories they wrote, let them know how they must go back and revise their drafts.

Why? Students often have a difficult time developing their stories or adding in details, because they don't know what they need. Using the summarizing strategy gives students a roadmap of their work. They need to revise their stories so that the questions can be answered by the reader.

Extension: This is actually an extension of summarizing in reading workshop. This technique also works with historical events, as I often have my students summarize what we're learning in social studies.

Working with Evolving Venn Diagrams

I truly appreciate a good ending. I love the end of *Walk Two Moons* by Sharon Creech (1996). It's a story about a little girl, Salamanca, who struggles with life without her mother. Her grandparents take her on a car trip to visit her mom, and throughout the trip, readers fall in love with Sal's grandparents. Her grandmother's cherished phrase is "huzza huzza." As the story progresses, readers get more and more attached to this trio. When tragedy strikes, Sal has to learn to live without her grandmother. I have told enough of the novel for teachers everywhere to be mad at me for giving away part of the ending, but I promise there are more surprises, and it is well worth the read. The novel ends with Sal accepting the changes in her life. The last words are: *Huzza Huzza.*

It's one of those books that make you sigh and say, "Mmm, that was good." A good ending should move the reader on to think about the character's next adventure or to have a sense of how the character's future may go.

Endings are hard for me and for my students to write. I have noticed that they often skip the ending, solving the problem with a one-sentence ending like, "It was all a dream." Yet there is nothing more satisfying for a writer than to nail an ending. I think the difficulty happens for several reasons. Mostly, kids are tired by the time they get to the end. I know I am. Yet it's a great feeling to end a piece as powerfully as you began it and to know it's done—that the reader will be left feeling satisfied. It's an area of teaching writing with which I have struggled to do a better job.

Maybe because it's the most difficult part of writing for me, it's also the most difficult thing for me to teach my children. I've worked hard at it, and have found a revising strategy that helps my students develop a more focused ending. I usually try this strategy midyear, after students are comfortable with and eloquent at summarizing their work.

Gathered around the easel, drafts and notebooks in hand, we begin. "I've noticed that you all do a great job summarizing your stories to make sure you have all the elements of plot."

"Does this mean we can stop doing that?" asks Joey. He's my shortcut man—any time he can find a shortcut, he'll take it.

"Well, not exactly. I think many of you summarize naturally as you write. You're thinking about the questions, making sure you have all the elements. Is that right?"

Heads nod. "I think we're ready for the next step. What I have noticed in your writing is that your endings are quite short. Has anyone noticed that about his or her own writing?"

Hands go up. "I'm tired and just want to get it done sometimes," admits one.

"I get tired too when I write. This next strategy is going to help you focus on your ending to develop it. You'll see that as you get better at developing other parts of your story, you will have more energy for the ending."

I draw a Venn diagram on the easel.

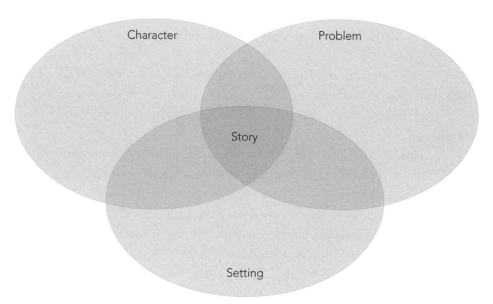

"These are the three basic things you need for a story. There needs to be a character, a setting and a problem," I say. "When you have all three of these together, then you're on your way to writing a story. Without an element, you don't have a complete plot."

"We know this, Ms. B," Joey reminds me.

"Right. If you're sure you have these things then you're ready for this next diagram."

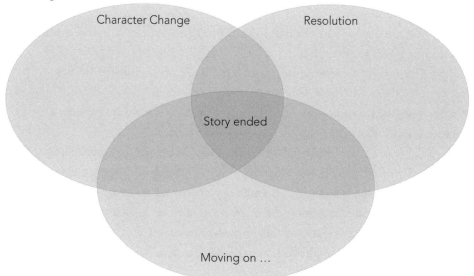

"Gosh, this looks like what we have been talking about in reading," Shannon comments.

"It is. As readers, we have noticed that the main characters usually change somehow throughout the book. There is a resolution to the problem, and a good ending gives the reader a sense that the character moves on with life.

"Now let's use these things as writers to make sure we're providing our readers with what they'll expect from a good story. Copy this Venn diagram into your notebooks."

When students are ready, I continue with the lesson. "What I want you to do today, before revising and move on to editing, is to make sure you answer these questions on the Venn diagram.

"Does your character change? In this circle, I want you to note how the character changes from the beginning of your story to the end. If you're not sure, go back and reread your story.

"Is the problem resolved? In this circle, I want you to write down how the problem is solved. This should only take a sentence. I don't need all of the details, I just want you to be sure you have indeed solved the problem.

"Finally, read your ending. Does it wrap up the story and give the reader a sense that the character moves on? This is hard. When I get to my endings, I often reread endings of books I really love, to get a sense of what I'm trying to do.

"If you are able to put notes down in all three circles, you can check the middle where they overlap."

"So, we do this in our notebooks and work on anything that's not done, right?" asks Matthew.

"Right. I'll come around and confer. You may want to work with a partner on this. Go write."

This is not an easy task. By midyear, most students have the character change and problem resolution down pat, but the ending and moving-on aspect continues to elude them. This strategy doesn't necessarily fix it, but it brings it to the writer's attention. Most students discover that they do not have a developed ending. As they talk with their partners, they begin to think through how the story should end to satisfy the reader.

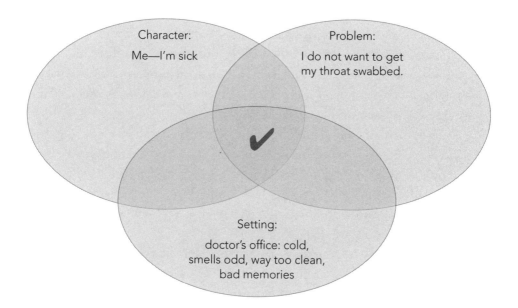

Using the overlapping circles allows the writer to envision how these three elements come together. In the example above, Colleen thinks through her scary visit to the doctor. This is a quick way to make sure she has the three elements of plot as well as the ending three elements for her story.

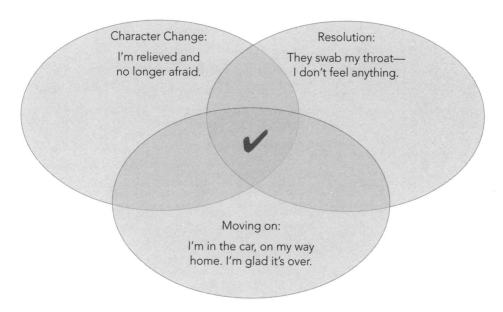

As a teacher, I sometimes have a strategy breakthrough. The light goes on and I think to myself, why haven't I always done this? And it's not that I'm doing something new and exciting, but rather that the strategy just makes sense to me ... finally. That's how I felt when I realized the strategies for reading comprehension could work for revising writing.

I had been thinking about the reading-writing connection a lot and was trying to access it, but mainly through reading like a writer—for craft. It was as if a light came on in my head in the middle of a reading lesson, as I asked my students, "What is the author trying to help us understand?" I suddenly realized I could ask the kids this in their writing, "What are you trying to help the reader understand and how are you doing this?"

Since then, my revising strategies have been more focused, like the ones I've shared. These help my students not only look at their writing more deeply and organize their thinking as writers, but also become much more aware of their audience.

As I continue to work with my students as readers and writers, I watch the boundaries between the workshops blur. My students constantly bring up their reading and their writing in each workshop. The writer's notebook no longer stays in the desk until writing time—writing time is all the time. Students constantly jot things in their notebooks or on Post-it notes to add to their notebooks whenever they read something they want to write about or emulate.

Once students realize that what they know as readers can help them as writers, they start to make those connections for themselves and keep reminders in their writer's notebooks. Skills blend, each influencing the others. That is what we want: writers who read and readers who write coming together in a notebook.

Chapter 6:

❦

Writing Wrongs: Editing, Spelling, and Punctuation

As a writer, I hate to be wrong. I want my editor to read my chapters once and say, "Marvelous. This is perfect, Aimee." (For the record, she never once said that after reading my writing for the first time.) Students are the same way. They want their writing to be marvelous and perfect the first time—the afraid-to-be-wrong syndrome rears its ugly head.

To make matters worse, teachers from all grade levels—even through high school—do not really talk much about the difference between editing and revision. So, many of my students see revision as changing spelling, punctuation, or capital letters.

While teaching at a writing institute this past summer, I had an interesting conversation with my teacher group. I had a mix of twenty-two teachers who taught grades four through twelve. These teachers were sharp—one of the better groups I have ever worked with.

I asked the teachers to work in groups to make two lists: One list for the things they want students to revise in their writing and the other list for things to do while editing. We came back together after ten minutes or so; our lists looked something like this:

Revision	Editing
Vary sentences	Check capitalization
Wording	Check ending punctuation and proper uses of commas
Add details	Check spelling
	Subject-verb agreement
	Paragraph structure
	Make sure verb tense is the same throughout the piece
	Edit passive voice
	Complete sentences—avoid run-on sentences and fragments

The editing list went on and on. As teachers, we sometimes are vague on exactly what we want kids to do when they revise. But we know exactly what we want from editing, as the lists show.

I began questioning this group of teachers. "What do you mean by 'vary sentences?'" I began.

"Don't start each sentence the same way," someone responded.

"I want students to vary the length of their sentences," another teacher added.

"Okay, this can mean two different things—or even more. I know I don't want my students to have the simple sentence structure throughout their whole piece," I replied. So as a group we started unpacking the revision list. We asked ourselves what we meant by each of these things we listed. We found there were a lot of expectations and not a lot of direct teaching.

One high school teacher said, "Our group realized two things. If we have been this vague in our teaching, no wonder students are editing instead of revising. And if we put the emphasis on editing, why would kids revise when they'll only have to edit yet again? So we decided we should spend more time on revision, and a lot of the editing will take care of itself as they reread and rewrite."

I love that comment and savor it. Our group nodded in agreement, realizing the truth in this conclusion. This is why the previous chapters are filled with lessons on revision, and why there are fewer lessons on editing in this chapter. As students take care in revising their writing, they also hone their editing skills.

Structural Lessons

In fourth grade, I teach paragraph structure. Most of my students have a sense of what a paragraph is—that it should have three to five sentences, blah, blah, blah. However, most students do not write naturally in paragraphs. Actually they write in what I lovingly call a "Bert Story" format. Remember Bert from Sesame Street, with the uni-brow across his forehead? My students' writing looks like Bert's eyebrow—one long paragraph, a uni-paragraph. Two- and three-page stories, but just one long paragraph.

Although there are the makings of several different paragraphs within their work, kids really struggle with knowing when to start a new paragraph. Somehow, telling them to start a new paragraph whenever they have a new topic confuses them. It's the old afraid-to-be-wrong syndrome.

The technique that I teach for this is not brain surgery. It's not even creative, but it does the trick. First, we have a mini-lesson reviewing what constitutes a paragraph and the "rules" for paragraphing (Figure 6–1).

Figure 6–1 *Rules of Thumb for Paragraphing*

1. In general, paragraphs are three to five sentences. Published writing often has more or less to a paragraph, but we're just learning to write, so stick with three to five sentences.

2. There are three basic parts to a paragraph. In general, you need all three. They are the topic sentence, detail sentences, and ending sentence.

3. Always, always, always *indent* the first sentence of a paragraph. An "indent" is about the length of the tip of your thumb to the first knuckle.

This review takes little time. My students tend to "know" paragraphs, they just don't know how to write them. Students keep notes in their notebooks toward the back. We may even paste in a couple of sample paragraphs that I have written or have copied from a book. Here is an example:

> *Children would eat better if they had healthier food choices at school. Students should have a fruit and a vegetable choice every day. Instead of cookies, the cafeteria should offer low-fat crackers. Also, a salad or other vegetarian dish should be offered as a daily choice. I think schools should ban junk food and offer healthier choices for lunch.*

Students then work with partners to prove this really is a paragraph. Basically, they check the work I give them to make sure there is one topic sentence, some supporting details, and a concluding sentence. Students use a green pencil to underline the topic sentence, a yellow pencil to underline the detail sentences, and a red pencil to underline the ending sentence (Figure 6–2).

Figure 6–2 *Editing Strategy: Understanding Paragraph Structure*

How: On a piece of chart paper, review the "Rules of Thumb" for paragraphs by listing and discussing each part. (See Figure 6–1.) Then, review or introduce the three parts of a paragraph: topic sentence, detail sentences, and ending sentence. Students should write this in the back of their notebooks. You could give them a copy of it already typed up; however, children pay more attention to things they need to write.

Next, give each student a copy of a paragraph that you have written or have copied from a text. Students glue this into their writer's notebooks. With a green pencil, students underline the topic sentence. With a yellow pencil, students underline the detail sentences. With a red pencil, students underline the ending sentence.

Why? This strategy helps them remember the three parts of the paragraph. Often students know in their heads what the parts of a paragraph are, but they cannot identify them in context. This gives them practice with a correctly written paragraph.

Extension: Have students write their own paragraphs in their notebooks on any topic. Then they can switch notebooks with a partner and try color-coding the paragraph.

This sounds very structured but is new for many of my students. Children find comfort in structure when they're uncomfortable. So this is where we start. This all takes place in the notebook. Then I tell the kids to look at their drafts from writing workshop, and if they notice they need to make some paragraphs, they should do so (Figure 6–3).

Figure 6–3 **Guidelines for Paragraph Edit**

1. Topic Sentence (Editing code: Green for start)
The topic sentence is your hook, it should have a bit of attitude in it. There is only one topic sentence per paragraph. For example, "My guinea pig is the best pet in the world."

2. Detail Sentences (Editing code: Yellow—slowing down to give information)
The detail sentences are your "proof" that your topic sentence is true. You are giving reasons to support your topic sentence. For example: "My guinea pig likes to cuddle. He likes to play with me. He even eats out of my hand."

3. Ending Sentence (Editing code: Red)
The ending sentence is your wrap-up. It ends the topic of the paragraph and may lead the reader to the next paragraph. For example: "I love my guinea pig."

Many students will need more help than this. I don't want the lesson to take a whole writer's workshop from their writing, so I work in bits and pieces. I think of these as a series of mini-lessons.

The second lesson about revising paragraphs helps lead the students to further revision. I start by asking for a student volunteer to put a paragraph from his or her writing on chart paper. As a class, we then underline any topic sentences in green. We underline detail sentences in yellow and any concluding sentences in red. I say "any" because sometimes we don't find one of these three kinds of sentences and sometimes we find more than just one topic or concluding sentence.

We then refer to our notes on paragraphs. In general, a paragraph should have one topic sentence. Check the chart paper—does this paragraph have one topic sentence? If not, how do we fix it? Does this paragraph have three or four detail sentences that relate to the topic sentence? If not, how do we fix it? We eventually fix the paragraph together. I then ask the students to try this out in their notebooks with a paragraph from their own writing.

It is amazing what the students discover. I love listening to their conversations. "Oh my gosh, I have no details anywhere—just topic sentences and conclusions." Or "I don't have one concluding sentence in my whole story. No wonder I can't get to an ending!"

Nicole found she had few details in her story. Once she tried this strategy in her notebook, she was able to recognize what she needed and where. (For the sake of this black-and-white book, the color code was changed to different kinds of lines: Dotted line for topic sentence, single underline for detail sentences, and double underline for concluding sentence.) Here is her sample from her notebook:

First paragraph:

My cousins are very weird. When they come over to my house, they laugh until they are sick. But, when I go to their house, they don't make a peep.

Nicole decided she didn't have enough detail sentences. Instead of my telling her to add more details to her story, Nicole knew she needed to add details to support her topic sentence, "My cousins are very weird."

Revised paragraph:

My cousins are very weird. When they come over to my house, they laugh until they are sick. They make funny noises while watching movies. My cousins even run in the house. But, when I go to their house, they don't make a peep.

Figure 6–4   *Editing Strategy: Color-Coding Paragraphs*

How: Students will use their current drafts of writing to revise paragraphs. First, they must determine if the paragraphs they have are correctly structured. Often students will have one long paragraph that needs to be broken into several small ones.

As students read through their drafts, they will underline any topic sentences in green. All detail sentences will be underlined in yellow (or black if using yellow legal pads), and ending sentences will be underlined in red.

After color-coding the paragraphs, students will have a visual representation of what they need to do. Do they have too many topic sentences without details? Did they forget wrap-up sentences? Students then go to revise paragraphs based on what they need.

Why? Oftentimes children don't know how to make their pieces longer or where to add details. This strategy helps kids see their paragraphs in parts. If there are not enough yellow lines between green and red ones, then that is where the writer needs to add details. This provides a road map for students to add to their writing.

Caution: When students don't understand what to do or are trying to do this without really doing it, they'll underline sentences without reading them. So, a child might underline the first sentence green, the next three yellow, and the fourth one red without thinking about how those sentences act within a paragraph. Then the student will repeat the pattern. If you see perfect paragraphing colors in a draft the first time, you might want to check to see if the child was simply creating the pattern. If so, the child did not understand what to do, doesn't understand paragraphs, or didn't want to do it. Whatever the case may be, teacher intervention is needed.

Students use this strategy on their drafts (Figure 6–4). What do they learn? They learn *where* to put more details. They learn *how* to separate and organize their ideas. They learn *when* it's okay to have paragraphs that are shorter or longer than the general three-to-five sentence rule.

Having the paragraph notes in their notebooks allows students to use this strategy again and again.

Playing with Grammar, Spelling, and Mechanics

Notebooks are useful for supporting editing, or "correcting" parts of writing, in many ways. During this phase, students are correcting grammar, usage, mechanics, and spelling. (My school system reduced this to the acronym GUMS.) Teaching grammar and spelling is an important part of teaching writing. I find it is more effective to teach this during a time when most of my students are editing.

The key to teaching quality editing is to take it one skill at a time. This is difficult to do, because there are so many mistakes that we see at first. However, kids can't master more than one thing at a time and truly remember it weeks, days, or even hours later. If they can, they should be encouraged to become editors.

For example, in fourth grade I expect my students to begin each sentence with a capital letter and end it with some form of punctuation. So I don't spend a lot of time on that. My students do struggle, however, with identifying and using passive voice. So I spend time on identifying passive verbs and replacing them with active ones.

Gathering the class together, I start a conversation by referring to work we have already done. "Boys and girls, remember our work with *John Henry?*" They nod and say, yes. "I want you to turn to our work in your notebooks that we did with this text. I'll give you a moment to find it."

Students soon flip to the right page and are skimming over their notes.

"What did we notice about the kinds of words Lester used to create images in the readers' minds?" I ask.

Hands go up, and Michael answers, "active verbs."

"Right. We noticed that Lester used verbs that showed action and created images, like *pulverized.*" I continue, "There are some verbs, though, that don't show action."

"How can that be?" Colleen asks, "I thought all verbs were action words."

"Verbs definitely drive the sentence, but can you show me how to *do* the verb *is?*" I ask.

Students look around at each other with a look that says, what in the world is she talking about? I begin to list some verbs on the board that lead to passive voice in writing. (We'll look at our grammar book in the next mini-lesson.) I list *is, are,* and *was.* Three overused forms of the verb *to be* in my students' writing.

"These are verbs." I say.

"Really?" asks Matthew. "I didn't know that."

"Yes, they are verbs. We use them a lot. The problem is we use them so much, we forget to use more active verbs."

"And then our writing doesn't have images, right?" interrupted Matthew.

"Sometimes, yes." I say. "Today, I want you to choose a notebook entry you have already written. Circle the words *is, are,* and *was.* Then try to rewrite the entry using more active verbs." And off they go to work (Figure 6–5).

Figure 6–5 *Editing Strategy: Identifying Passive Voice*

How: Students are working in the back of the notebook, where they keep their grammar and editing notes. As I begin the lesson, I may refer to the *John Henry* example we used earlier when reading like writers. In that example we noticed the author used verbs to create images more than he used adjectives. I may even review the list we created to show them the kinds of verbs the author used: *pulverized, shook, draped,* and *glimmered.* These are action verbs. You can do these things—they create images of activity in your mind.

Then either take out the grammar book and turn to the linking verbs and forms of *to be,* or begin listing some of them on the board: *is, were, was, will, would, should, are,* etc. Ask the students if these words create images in their minds. Can you actively do them? Show me *is.* You can't. These verbs create a passive voice. Have students make a list of these in their notebooks with a heading: Try NOT to Use These.

Why? Writers create images in readers' minds. They do so with strong verbs and specific nouns. The verb drives the sentence, so it can be the most important word in a sentence. Students should be aware of the weaker verbs—passive verbs—that don't add to their writing. Passive voice may not be avoided altogether, but it can be decreased significantly with some attention.

Extension: Give students a paragraph using passive voice to glue into their notebooks. Working with a partner, students circle the weak verbs and replace them with active verbs. Finally, have students focus in their writing on using active voice.

The most glaring errors, however, are spelling errors. Sometimes misspelled words are hard to find, and, if you think one is misspelled, well, then you have to correct it. That's even more work. And quite frankly, writers are tired by this point; they want it done and over with already. For these reasons, among others, I make sure to share several strategies for finding misspelled words with my students. They can choose one that works for them.

A series of editing mini-lessons about finding misspelled words may begin something like this. Keep in mind that I start a lesson, kids take notes in their notebooks, try it out on a sample I give them or on an entry in their notebooks, and finally go to their drafts.

I start with a question: How do you know when a word is misspelled in your writing? The answers come back at me: "They don't look right." "I circle words I use that I know I don't know how to spell." "I just read through my story and look for words that aren't right."

Kids are writing this question and their answers in their notebooks while I write them on the chart paper. I then hand them a paragraph to glue into their notebooks and direct them to try using these strategies to find the misspelled words in the passage. I'll have this same passage on an overhead transparency so we can look at it together. As we go through the passage to share the "answers," a few students may get all of the misspelled words; however, many will miss words they should have known were misspelled.

This is not uncommon. The more proficient we become at reading the more we focus on comprehension rather than spelling. It's only when a misspelled word interrupts comprehension that many of us will even notice it. This doesn't excuse misspelled words in published pieces, but it does help explain why it's difficult for students to find all of the mistakes.

I then ask the students to read the passage backward, isolating each word from the context of the story. So we start at the end of the sample, with the last word, and read from right to left. This forces kids to look at each word by itself. "Do you notice possible misspellings? If so, circle them. Then go back and read through the piece from the beginning. Circle any more words you think are incorrect. Then go back and correct the spellings." The following sample is written the way we would read it backward. It won't make sense, but you'll see all of the misspellings.

> .bed in up woke I Then .home get to how know didnt I becus
> ,cryed and cryed I .lost got and woods the through walkd I
> .dreem bad a had I nite Last

Figure 6–6   *Editing Strategy: Reading Backwards*

Reading Backwards (to find misspelled words)

How: Give students a passage of text to glue into their notebooks. There should be several misspelled words in the text.
  Show students how to read the paragraph backward in order to isolate each word. Tell them to start at the end, and read right to left. Looking at each word, they should determine if it is spelled correctly. If they're not sure or know it's wrong, they should circle it.
  After students have had a chance to complete the exercise, go over the words they should have caught. Using this strategy in their own writing will help them find misspelled words.

Why? As students become more fluent readers, they begin to read for meaning instead of pronouncing each individual word. This is good for reading, but it can cause the reader not to pay as close attention to each word. So, when students go to edit their work or work of others, they use what they know about reading and often miss words spelled incorrectly. By reading the text backward, it won't make sense, students will go more slowly, and they'll focus on each word in an isolated way.

Extension: Read text backward to find homophones (words that sound alike but are spelled differently). Circle the homophones. Then go back and read the text for meaning. Is the circled word the correct homophone for the sentence? If it is...great. If not, fix it.

After students try this in their notebooks, I hear a lot of "OHHH! Now I get it." Students then go to their drafts to find those misspellings using this strategy (Figure 6–6).

Ending Punctuation Review

After I read the poem "Call the Periods, Call the Commas" in one breath, someone usually says, "That's a hard poem to read." It is a hard poem to read aloud. There are no line breaks, white space, or punctuation to guide or give the reader pause. This is not unlike some of my students' work, especially in the beginning of the year.

●C Call the Periods
Call the Commas

Call the doctors Call the nurses Give me a breath of
air I've been reading all your stories but the periods
aren't there Call the policemen Call the traffic guards
Give me a STOP sign quick Your sentences are running
When they need a walking stick Call the commas Call
the question marks Give me a single clue Tell me
where to breathe with a punctuation mark or two

(Dakas 1990, p. 49)

"It is a difficult poem. Kalli Dakos used to be a teacher. Why do you think she wrote this?"

Hands go up everywhere. "It's pretty obvious," says Shannon, "she wanted her students to use punctuation."

"Right, and why do you suppose I gave this to all of you today?" I ask. Now kids are giggling guiltily as they realize what I'm going to tell them. I continue, "I know you know about ending punctuation and basic comma usage. I need you to practice what you know in all of your writing—no matter where it is—in your notebook, in social studies, on science labs … everywhere."

Students seem resigned to the mini-lecture, but I'm not through yet. The next day, I continue the review with a chart drawn on paper (see Figure 6–7):

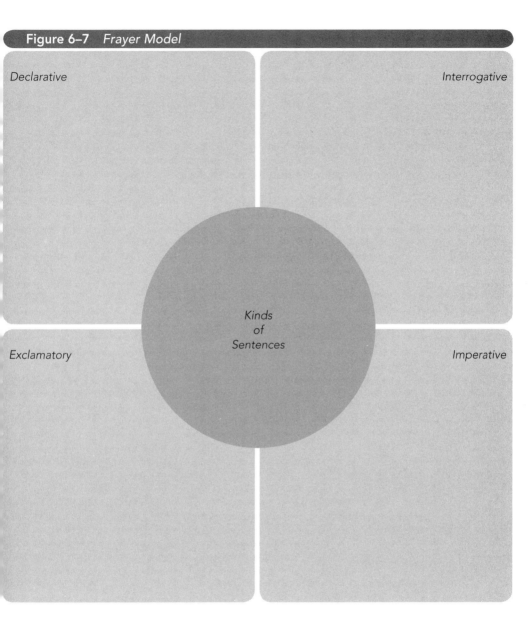

Figure 6–7 *Frayer Model*

Declarative

Interrogative

Exclamatory

Imperative

Kinds
of
Sentences

This is known as a Frayer Model. "Boys and girls, I want to make sure we're all on the same page concerning end punctuation."

I review the four kinds of sentences: declarative (a simple statement), interrogative (a question), exclamatory (an exclamation), and imperative (a command). I then ask, "What kind of punctuation do you use to end each of

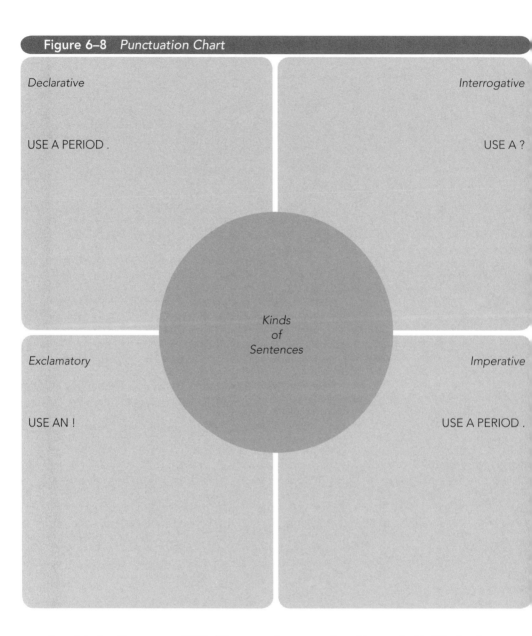

Figure 6–8 *Punctuation Chart*

Declarative

USE A PERIOD .

Interrogative

USE A ?

Kinds
of
Sentences

Exclamatory

USE AN !

Imperative

USE A PERIOD .

these kinds of sentences?" We fill in our chart together (Figure 6–8). We finish
the review by hanging the chart in the classroom as a reference. This is the extent
of my whole-class review on ending punctuation in fourth grade. If smaller
groups of students need more instruction, I usually use conferences to help them
individually (Figure 6–9).

Figure 6–9   *Editing Strategy: Ending Punctuation Review*

How: By third grade, students have been taught, reminded, and told to use capital letters at the beginning of sentences and ending punctuation at the end of sentences. But they don't always use that punctuation, do they? As a review, I give each child a copy of the poem "Call the Periods, Call the Commas," by Kalli Dakos. They glue it in their notebooks as I read it aloud. (This poem takes practice because it looks like a paragraph and there is NO ending punctuation anywhere.) As kids are giggling at my face turning blue, they get the point. I'll ask, "What does this poem tell us?" And clearly, students know it's a reminder to use ending punctuation: periods, question marks, and exclamation points. This can also lead into a series of lessons about comma usage.

Why? Kids still don't use ending punctuation like they should, and it's a funny way to get a serious point across.

Extensions: This lesson can open a series of lessons about commas. Or it can start a series of lessons about types of sentences and correct ending punctuation: declarative sentences get periods, interrogative sentences get question marks, exclamatory sentences get exclamation points, and compound sentences get commas and periods.

Punctuating Compound Sentences

My students are seated at their desks where they can see the overhead. Notebooks are opened to the back because we will begin discussing how to punctuate compound sentences. Students generally take notes by writing in their notebooks while I write on the overhead.

"The past couple of days we have talked about ending punctuation," I begin. "Who can give us a quick summary as a review?"

"Ending punctuation comes at the end of a sentence, question, or exclamation. A period, question mark, or exclamation point are the only three ways to end a sentence," volunteers Courtney. From the way she regurgitates the information, I wonder if maybe I've harped on the point too much this week.

"Right. But, like any rule, there is an exception," I say.

"There is?!" blurts Nate. "I thought that was a done deal."

"Well, it's true that you must always have some sort of ending punctuation after a complete sentence, but it can sometimes be a comma instead of a period. Does anyone know when you would use a comma and not a period?"

"In a compound sentence?" answers Courtney, a bit unsure of herself.

"Yes, that's exactly it." I begin to write on the overhead as students write in their notebooks:

Punctuation for Compound Sentences

Rules:

●◆ A sentence must always have ending punctuation.

●◆ A sentence may end with a comma within a compound sentence.

●◆ A compound sentence must end with standard ending punctuation.

Example:

David runs very fast. David likes to paint.

David runs very fast, and David likes to paint.

I stop to talk with the students. "What is the difference between the two examples?"

Matthew is first to raise his hand. "You use the same sentences but you put a comma after *fast,* then the word *and.*"

"Good observation. When you write a compound sentence, you have two sentences. The first sentence can't use a period so you need to use a comma. Notice the comma comes before the word *and.*" For some reason my students often want to put the comma after the word *and* or *but.* I have found that making this simple connection between the period and comma is very helpful in clearing up that misunderstanding (Figure 6–10).

Figure 6–10 *Editing Strategy: Punctuating Compound Sentences*

How: Refer back to the poem, "Call the Periods, Call the Commas," by Kalli Dakos. It's important to have ending punctuation, but sometimes one sentence is so long it needs some rest stops.

In the back of the notebook, students copy the sentences I have written on the board: "Ms. Buckner likes to read. Ms. Buckner thinks reading is good for the soul." Two separate sentences can be joined into one sentence by using a connecting word: *and, but, because, so, or.* When you join two sentences to make a compound sentence, you need to put a comma where the period would usually go. For example (students write this in their notebooks, too, making the comma bold): "Ms. Buckner likes to read, because she thinks it is good for the soul."

Notice, where the period used to be after "Ms. Buckner likes to read," there is now a comma. That allows the reader to take a breath and signals there is more to come. In a compound sentence, you may have only one comma for separating sentences. If you have more than one, you may have a run-on sentence.

Have students try this with a partner by writing three compound sentences of their own (in their notebooks) and punctuating them correctly.

Figure 6–10 *Editing Strategy: Punctuating Compound Sentences*

Why? Students often want to put the comma in a compound sentence after the connecting word. By demonstrating that it goes where the period should have gone, this lesson helps kids remember to put the comma before the connecting word. For those who aren't using commas at all, it's a good way to introduce the skill.

Extensions: Students can edit an entry in their notebooks for commas in compound sentences. Have students rewrite an entry from their notebooks and combine several pairs of sentences into compound sentences. Use the commas correctly. This lesson can also lead to a series about varying sentence length in a piece.

The question comes to mind, Do we ever *really* become independent writers? I am beginning to think—not if we're lucky. Although I want my students to have the ability to write independently, without me telling them what and when to write, I also want them to understand that writers evolve, as we all do. They need to be open to the opportunities that will improve their writing. Some of these may come from being in a community of writers, like in our classrooms. Some may come from working with partners and learning how to talk about writing. Some may come from using resources to inform themselves of the correctness or structure of their writing.

Editing is a lot of work. It can make a mess of a draft—to the point where writers can no longer read it. Using the writer's notebook to support this work gives students a place to try their revisions and hone their editing skills before making changes to their drafts. It's not that the draft doesn't ever get messy, but it's now a more productive mess.

Chapter 7:

Assessing the Notebook

Grades. Test scores. They're so intertwined with education that for some it's unthinkable to not grade something. Yet, how would you grade a notebook as personal as the one I've described in this book? How can children separate grading their notebooks from grading their lives? Should we even grade notebooks or just the finished products?

These are questions that I've wrestled with over the past decade, and that have influenced my decisions about assessing the notebooks. Because I teach fourth grade, with grades on the report card, my practice is to grade the notebook. I wouldn't recommend this particular process for younger grades. It is, however, a process I have used in middle school as well as in my current fourth-grade position.

Randy Bomer, author of *Time for Meaning* (1995), helped answer my assessment questions. I value the notebook, as my students know from my actions and expectations. Yet in other subjects, we send the message of what we value by what we grade or what we put on the test. I went through school valuing what would be graded and what would be tested over other things. I learned quickly what I could get away with and what I couldn't when doing work for different teachers. It's part of the student game—know what that teacher wants and do it.

Because I value the notebook as a learning process, it's logical that I would want to assess student progress. With computerized grade books, anecdotal reports are more difficult to translate into a grade. Given these restraints, the ideas from Randy's book, and a thoughtful colleague, Christy Malko, a writer's notebook rubric has emerged.

This rubric helps parents know what is expected of students. It helps students know and understand how this translates into progress. It helps me focus my assessment of the notebook on qualities that I know will lead to better writing. I have seen dozens of notebook and writing rubrics and checklists. Each reflects what the teacher values. I show you the rubric I use and how I use it. It will be up to you to consider these questions as you develop your own rubric:

What do you value about the notebook?
What are the most important qualities of writing you are looking to develop with the notebook?

Taking Bomer's lead, I focus on three aspects of keeping a notebook (see Figure 7–1).

Fluency and Flexibility

Writers write a lot on some days and very little on others. They write about different topics and they write in different ways. A notebook should be a mixture of ideas, styles, and lengths. This part of the grade looks at the lengths of the entries in relation to their completeness. Are most of the entries finished, or are most only a few sentences long, leaving thoughts unwritten? That is, does the writer stop abruptly at the end of the page or is she or he willing to continue the entry to another page and a good stopping place? Does the writer practice strategies from class? Does the writer try new writing approaches demonstrated in mini-lessons? Does the writer write about a variety of topics or are the entries only about one thing?

I had a student who wrote only about Dodge trucks. He wrote what seemed like the same thing over and over. Another student wrote only about football. Every Monday I got the play-by-play of the Sunday games. On Tuesday I got the recap of the Monday night game. On Wednesday through Friday I got predictions and pregame analysis. I was thrilled when football season ended that year! The Dodge writer did not show any flexibility of topic or style. The football writer at least did some thoughtful reflection on the teams, but the topic followed a rote pattern of writing. This is what I'm trying to break kids from in their writing.

Figure 7–1   *Writer's Notebook Evaluation Rubric*

Grade	A	B	C	D
Flexibility and Fluency	Most entries are completed. Writer uses a variety of strategies and topics.	Many entries are completed. Writer uses strategies from class and shows some topic variety.	Entries are left unfinished. Topics and strategies may vary.	Entries are underdeveloped. Little or no variety in writing strategies.
Thoughtfulness	Entries are thoughtful and reflective, revealing new insights to the writer's thinking. Writer practices proper grammar, usage, mechanics, and spelling (GUMS).	Entries tend to be thoughtful. They may reveal new insights to the writer's thinking. A pattern of topics develops over a number of entries. Writer practices proper GUMS.	Entries resemble a diary format or bed-to-bed-type stories. Little or no reflective thinking is evident. Writer does not give attention to GUMS.	Entries are difficult to read due to handwriting and/or GUMS. Writer does not demonstrate reflective thinking.
Frequency	90 percent of required entries.	80 percent of required entries.	74 percent of required entries.	70 percent of required entries.

Thoughtfulness

This is the scariest part of the rubric for me. It's the most subjective part of the rubric. As a teacher, I am so used to being called on the carpet for every decision I make that I've gotten used to having "evidence" to support all my thinking. I realized, though, that as an adult who works with this age group 180 days a year, I have a good sense of what is thoughtful work and what is not. I can even show sample entries to demonstrate the differences if "evidence" is necessary. I tell my students that any entry that reads like a grocery list is not thoughtful. For example, an entry about going to an amusement park that starts with waking up, eating breakfast, riding in the car, getting tickets, waiting in line for the roller coaster, and so on is a grocery-list entry. Some teachers at my school refer to this as a bed-to-bed entry—it starts when the student wakes up and ends when the student goes to bed.

This is the most subjective part of the notebook grade. But then, writing *is* subjective, with no way of putting percentages on each and every element. Sharing a lot of notebook samples that demonstrate thoughtful writing helps guide even the most struggling of writers.

The following student samples demonstrate a thoughtful entry and an entry that is not as thoughtful:

●◆ Am I Ready for Fifth Grade? by Davis 8-24

Am I ready for fifth grade? I mean, it's takin a big step. There will be tougher classes, more homework. The next thing I know, I'm doing math I've never dreamed of doing and reading books 14 chapters long. Will I make good grades? Will the teacher like me? Will the tests be too hard or will I blow through it like Speedy Gonzalez? Maybe I'll just focus on fourth grade right now.

In this entry, Davis' anxiety about fifth grade is made clear by his rambling questions. Note the date: he just started fourth grade. He is specific about his concerns and about the things he expects to do. This is a rather thoughtful entry for a fourth grader in the second week of school.

●◆ When I Went Fishing With My Grandpa by Davis 8-30

It was a cool, September day. I caught 16 fish. One was a foot long and about four pounds. My brother went with us. I stuck my grandpa two times.

This entry is by the same child a few days later. Clearly, it's not as thoughtful as his previous entry. It simply recalls things that happened that day and who was there.

GUMS

Another aspect of this rubric is the GUMS grade. GUMS is the acronym my county uses to describe Grammar, Usage, Mechanics, and Spelling. I do not grade these by marking up the students' notebooks and pointing out all of their errors. Quite frankly, you would find mistakes in my notebook. What I look at is whether the writer practices what he or she knows about good writing. For instance, does the writer try to use a variety of words even if he or she is unsure of the spelling?

I expect fourth graders to spell the words *they* and *because* correctly on a regular basis. I also expect ending punctuation and a capitalized *I* when used as a pronoun. If the writer misses once in awhile, I don't worry. If it's constantly being missed, then I grade accordingly on the rubric and write the student a quick note about it. Just because I don't take my red pen and bleed over their notebook entries, does not mean I don't expect best practice. But then again, "practice" is the key word.

Frequency

I expect students to write … a lot. I don't check to see if they wrote at home every night. I collect notebooks about twice a month in the beginning of the year and about once a month toward the end.

I keep track of how many days are between my assessments, and expect one entry for each day of writer's workshop—even though they may write more than one entry that day—and three home entries per week. (My expectation is that students write at home at least three days a week. Many end up writing more; some do the minimum.) The entries must be dated and the ones written at home must have an asterick or an *H* written by the date. I then count. If I'm on a two-week rotation, the students should have the required sixteen entries (ten school days plus three days per week at home). I simply take a percentage of the entries they do have compared to the entries they should have and come up with the rubric grade. It's the easiest A they'll ever earn.

One Grade

Using this rubric as my guide, I can average the grades for each criterion and come up with one notebook grade. So, if a student gets an A for flexibility and fluency, an A for thoughtfulness, and a B for frequency, their overall grade is an A.

I know the rubric people may be curling their toes right now as they read this. I recognize that the purpose of rubrics is to look at qualities of writing and not to put a letter grade on it. I work in a county, however, that has used writing rubrics appropriately for the past decade, and parents are still asking, "… is this an A?" I think we bear some responsibility to make our assessments user friendly in a common language. Parents and students understand A, B, C, and D. I could easily put Excellent, Above Average, Average, Below Average on the rubric as well. The kids would still ask, though, "Is this an A?" I decided to sidestep this particular battle by putting letters at the top of the rubric. I feel the rest of the process of using a rubric to look at qualities of writing is still intact. It's worked for me, with few problems translating it to parents and students.

In the Beginning

The beginning of the year creates some complications with this assessment process. Most children keep a notebook for the first time in my class. Student writing may be superficial at first, so I do a lot of the guiding as students learn to reflect and use their notebooks.

It's important to read and assess the notebooks even at this stage. In the beginning, students need cheerleaders. They don't value their own writing, so we need to value it for them. Lucy Calkins once said, "Lean into your students' writing and say WOW. Even if there isn't a lot of wow there." As teachers, we need to see the possibilities in student work, we need to convince them they have a voice and important things to say, and we need to encourage them to keep working in the notebook.

I use the same rubric throughout the year. I interpret it a bit differently as we progress through the year because as students evolve as writers, so do the expectations. The most difficult part of the rubric, even at the beginning of the year, continues to be the thoughtfulness piece. Yet this is the most important part of the rubric; the whole point of keeping a writer's notebook is to be thoughtful.

When a student is thoughtful, revealing new insights to his or her writing, the entry reflects the effort the student puts into it. It may demonstrate new insights as applying a particular strategy helps the student explore his life in writing.

Look at these two examples of best life events:

List A	List B
1. I went to Disney World	1. The day my baby brother was born
2. I went to the beach	2. When I finished my first dance recital and my dad gave me flowers
3. I went to my grandma's house	3. When I found my dog after he had run away

List A shows a child who wrote about very general things. The writing from this list will be general, like a grocery list. It's okay to have one or two general things on the list, but the point is to really think about the good times in one's life. List B notes very specific events. More thought went into this list. It could have read, "my first dance recital" and "my dog."

When considering the thoughtfulness of the whole notebook, consider strategies in tandem with the writing it leads to later. So if the child wrote a thoughtful entry about going to Disney World, then the fact that his list wasn't as thoughtful would not be a big deal. The key to teaching thoughtful writing is model, model, model. Have students share their work, make overheads of thoughtful entries, and discuss them with your class. What you're looking for should not be a secret; kids need examples.

Too much of our assessment of learning looks at one entry, one piece of writing isolated in time. There is a place for that kind of assessment, but there is also a need for assessing the growth of a writer. One of the most important aspects of using a writer's notebook with students is to help them continually reflect on their growth and change as writers. So assessment doesn't just lie with me and the rubric. I encourage my students to reread their notebooks often. We take time to reflect on what they notice—how their writing is improving and what changes they see in how they approach the notebook.

Looking Back

◖◗ *Tori: If you look back at page 26 and read, I have lots and lots of spelling mistakes! It's not even funny now when I go back to read it, it looks like a two year old wrote it! The first sentence made me crack up. It was funny because I was such in a rush my sentences didn't make sense. How I went from my name to my friends from my friends to my guinea pig from my guinea pig to may blanket ... WOW! I was in a totally different world!*

Have you ever noticed the weird twitches students have when you ask them to check their work? I can envision their eyebrows moving as I ask, "Did you reread this to see if it makes sense?" It's like a death sentence to fourth graders. Reread and redo seem synonymous to them. But rereading their work is what writers do, and this is an important part of the evaluation process.

As a writer, I have found that I, too, hate rereading my own work. It's helpful to have time between writing and rereading. What makes rereading bearable for me is knowing the purpose. There are times we reread to find editing errors. There are times we reread for revisions. But, writers also reread their work to reflect on their writing, to see where they have been.

> Courtney: Keeping a writer's notebook helps me because it shows me what I might really like to write about. It also helps me become a better writer, because it shows me how well I'm doing.

Frequently, I have students take some writing time to reread their notebooks from cover to cover. If they have more than one notebook, they read them all. The purpose is for them to reflect on their writing. Students often notice how much their mechanics have improved. They notice the kinds of writing they like to do (fiction, nonfiction, poems, etc.). It is valuable for children to recognize themselves as writers in their own right. I don't say, "everyone write poetry," yet some kids will have poems sprinkled throughout their notebooks. I haven't said, "everyone write about your favorite toy or your favorite sports team," and yet notebooks are filled with just that. The notebooks are as different as the writers who are writing them.

> Cameron: I write lots of different things in my notebook. I don't focus on one type of writing though. … I practice different writing skills in it. I can write anything I want in here and that helps me to work on fiction stories, nonfiction stories and other things.

> Ashley: My notebook, to me, is the only thing I write in. Sure I never want to write, but sometimes I'm hooked. I can't stop writing. My notebook is filled with my thoughts and stories. It even has a rhyming poem.

Students often see more in their notebooks than I do. They become attached to their notebooks as they put more and more work into them day after day. Finishing a notebook is cause for celebration, but it's also a good-bye in some ways.

> Meredith: I feel nervous. I don't know why. I feel as if I've been cheated. Even though I have filled these pages with love and feeling. I'm so nervous. Are you supposed to feel this way? I think I need Ms. Buckner here to tell me all this. How am I supposed to act? Did the others feel this? I want do my last page in my favorite spot, here, next to Julie, Mack and Patrick., three of my best friends. My heart is pounding. Faster and faster. I'm shaking. I'm stalling. I don't want to leave. Now I know I'm a real author … Like Ms. Buckner always says, last words are the most important. Here we go!
> Huzza, Huzza!
> Alpha and Omega!
> Good Bye!

Formal Self-Evaluations

Toward the middle of the year, I ask the students to do a formal evaluation on their notebooks and writing progress. This is to help them think more deeply about where they started as writers, where they are now, and where they want to go. This project also helps students realize which strategies work best for them and what they need to continue to work on.

I adapted the following project from Joanne Hindley's book *In the Company of Children* (1996). Students are asked several questions about their notebooks and writing. After responding, students go through their notebooks and find entries that support their evaluation. Students mark these pages with sticky notes and either a parent volunteer or I make copies of the entries. (I have been known to bring my entire class down to the copy room so that we can make the copies.) Students then put the entries and their responses together in the form of a report—all very formal and official looking. At the end of the evaluation, students are asked to write a writing goal for the rest of the year (Figure 7–2). Figure 7–2 is also included in the appendix.

Figure 7–2 *Midyear Self-Evaluation*

Name _____

As a community of writers, we understand the tremendous energy it takes to write thoughtfully, to dig deep in our gut and get the story out. Sometimes our energy is zapped from our system and it takes a lot of concentration to write just one paragraph. It's a hard life—the life of a writer.

　　　Our writer's notebooks are filled with good writing and some not-so-good writing. Use your notebook to help you think about yourself as a writer. Reread your writer's notebook and comment on how you use the notebook and your commitment to it. (Do you write regularly? Do you write thoughtful entries? Is it a place you use to figure out the world around you? etc.)

_____

_____

_____

_____

_____

Midyear Evaluation Part 2

Make Your Own Decision

Part of a writer's job is making decisions about his or her own writing. Use your notebook and what you know about writing to make the selections below. Follow the directions carefully. Cross out each direction after you have finished it.

• Select two entries from your notebook you think best demonstrate that you are an original thinker. Mark them with sticky notes for copying. Attach the copies to this evaluation.

• Select two entries showing that you understand the qualities of good writing. Put sticky notes on these entries for copying. When you get the copies back, explain how these entries demonstrate good writing. Write your comments on the back of each copied entry. Attach them to the evaluation.

• Reread the entries you have selected and what you wrote about yourself as a writer. Then respond to the following questions.

1. From your rereading, selecting, and reflecting on your writing, what have you learned about yourself as a writer?

_____

_____

_____

_____

_____

_____

2. What topics do you tend to write about? (What are your writing patterns?)

_____

_____

_____

_____

_____

3. Think about yourself as a writer from the beginning of the year to now. How have you changed as a writer this year?

_____

_____

_____

_____

_____

4. What would you like to improve about your writing? Set a goal for yourself and write it below.

_____

_____

_____

_____

_____

Additional Comments:

The goals can focus on any area of writing in which they want to improve. We'll then monitor the goals for the rest of the year. If this is done at the end of the school year, students present their project to me in a conference and we decide their final grade together (Figure 7–3). Figure 7–3 can also be found in the appendix.

Figure 7–3 *End-of-Year Self-Assessment*

Name _____

Looking Back

This year we have focused on developing as readers and writers. Today you will be looking back over your work from this year. As readers and writers, it is important for us to know how we can improve, but it is also important for us to know how we *have* improved throughout the year. Use your writer's notebook and any other writing pieces from this school year to help you respond to the questions below.

1. What do good writers do?

_____
_____
_____
_____
_____

2. How would you describe yourself as a writer in the beginning of the year?

_____
_____
_____
_____
_____

3. How would you describe yourself as a writer now?

_____
_____
_____
_____
_____

4. Comment on how using a writer's notebook has helped you this year.

_____
_____
_____
_____
_____

5. Include three notebook entries—one from the beginning, middle, and end of the year—to show your progress. On sticky notes, point out how your writing improves throughout the year.

6. What revision techniques have you found work best for you?

_____
_____
_____
_____
_____

Include a piece of finished writing that shows that you used one of the techniques mentioned above.

7. What have you learned about editing this year?

_____
_____
_____
_____
_____

8. As a writer, during which part of the process do you write best? Explain.

_____
_____
_____
_____
_____

9. Using the rubric, evaluate your writer's notebook below:

      Flexibility and Fluency: _____
      Thoughtfulness: _____
      Frequency: _____
      Overall Score: _____

Additional Comments:

10. Considering all of this information, what grade do you believe best describes your writing performance this fourth quarter? Explain your reasoning. Remember you will share this evaluation with me and together we'll determine your grade.

_____
_____
_____
_____
_____

Here are some excerpts from Meredith's end-of-year self-evaluation:

Q: How would you describe yourself as a writer at the beginning of the year?

At the beginning of the year I knew nothing about writing. I didn't have a BM and E (beginning, middle and end). I wrote about anything. That was probably the biggest thing, I just pulled something out of the blue. I didn't know anything about writing.

Q: How would you describe yourself as a writer now?

I take something that happened in my life and write about it in my notebook. If it works for me, I make it into a story. My spelling has gotten better, and I've found I have a lot more feeling in my writing.

Q: Comment on how using a writer's notebook has helped you this year.

One thing I have noticed in my writer's notebook is that at one period of time I will have a lot of things to write about. And then a couple of pages later … I'll write about nothing. Another thing I have done, on accident, is I will write about something as little as finishing my notebook and will end up folding the page over. I like to write in funny places like outside in the rain, under a chair or next to a window. I think I can write very powerful entries.

One sample entry Meredith included to support her reflections follows:

There is one thing I will never forget. My friend told me her grandmother had cancer and was dying. We were on the playground talking about it. All of a sudden, out of nowhere, she said, "I wonder what my grandma's last words are going to be." Neither of us said a word.

    That evening, as my mom and I drove home, I thought about what she had said. I could not get it out of my head. When we got home, my dad had just hung up the phone. He told me Julia's grandma had died at 4:02 p.m.

Meredith later writes under this entry: "Some people would not pay attention if someone they knew said this. I did, because I'm a writer."

This evaluation seems very structured for the notebooks, which have been so flexible to writers. It's important, however, to structure the unknown for students. As they do the informal evaluations in the notebook, I ask simple questions like: How is keeping a notebook going for you? What are some strategies you find helpful? Using the rubric, how do you think you're doing in the notebook?

To think deeply and to provide examples takes time and some direction. Usually it takes my students about four or five days to complete the formal evaluation. It's a lot of time, but well worth it.

Final Thoughts

The best way for anyone to become a better writer is to write a lot. The writer's notebook not only provides a place for students to create writing, but also serves as a practice area for revisions and as a reference for editing. As students take ownership of the notebook—writing off strategies instead of prompts, filling it with life, not fantasy, writing about what is important to them—they become engaged writers. Engaged writers are willing to write more, and by writing more they get better at it.

All too often, elementary teachers are expected to be experts at everything. We're expected to know how to teach a child to read, to multiply and divide, to conduct a science experiment and read a time line. We're comfortable with a lot of it and manage with the rest. But there is good news when it comes to teaching writing. It's a secret that I'm willing to share …

You only have to write a little bit better than your students to "know" more about writing than your students. You don't have to be an expert. You can let the writer's notebook lead the way for each writer in your class, with you as the guide. The writing will happen, it will get better, and you will learn along with your students the excitement that comes from having filled a notebook and the true joy from having written well.

Appendix

Considerations for Notebooks

What kind of notebook are you considering: spiral, composition, binder, notepad, other?

Is it easily portable to take home and bring back to school?	
Does it provide a standard-sized page?	
Is it easily replaceable?	
Is it a size that will be easy for you to collect and read?	
Do you have a plan for where students will put their class notes and/or handouts?	
Will students be able to personalize the notebook?	
Is it important to take pages in and out of the notebook? Does your notebook support this?	
Is the notebook easy for all students to manage?	

Charting Author Style

Author	Style	Example	Text Reference

Midyear Self-Evaluation

Name _____

As a community of writers, we understand the tremendous energy it takes to write thoughtfully, to dig deep in our gut and get the story out. Sometimes our energy is zapped from our system and it takes a lot of concentration to write just one paragraph. It's a hard life—the life of a writer.

Our writer's notebooks are filled with good writing and some not-so-good writing. Use your notebook to help you think about yourself as a writer. Reread your writer's notebook and comment on how you use the notebook and your commitment to it. (Do you write regularly? Do you write thoughtful entries? Is it a place you use to figure out the world around you? etc.)

_____
_____
_____
_____
_____

Midyear Evaluation Part 2

Make Your Own Decision

Part of a writer's job is making decisions about his or her own writing. Use your notebook and what you know about writing to make the selections below. Follow the directions carefully. Cross out each direction after you have finished it.

• Select two entries from your notebook you think best demonstrate that you are an original thinker. Mark them with sticky notes for copying. Attach the copies to this evaluation.

• Select two entries showing that you understand the qualities of good writing. Put sticky notes on these entries for copying. When you get the copies back, explain how these entries demonstrate good writing. Write your comments on the back of each copied entry. Attach them to the evaluation.

• Reread the entries you have selected and what you wrote about yourself as a writer. Then respond to the following questions.

1. From your rereading, selecting, and reflecting on your writing, what have you learned about yourself as a writer?

_____
_____
_____
_____
_____

2. What topics do you tend to write about? (What are your writing patterns?)

_____
_____
_____
_____
_____
_____
_____

3. Think about yourself as a writer from the beginning of the year to now. How have you changed as a writer this year?

_____
_____
_____
_____
_____
_____

4. What would you like to improve about your writing? Set a goal for yourself and write it below.

_____
_____
_____
_____
_____
_____

Additional Comments:

End-of-year Self-Assessment

Name _____

Looking Back

This year we have focused on developing as readers and writers. Today you will be looking back over your work from this year. As readers and writers, it is important for us to know how we can improve, but it is also important for us to know how we *have* improved throughout the year. Use your writer's notebook and any other writing pieces from this school year to help you respond to the questions below.

1. What do good writers do?

_____
_____
_____
_____
_____

2. How would you describe yourself as a writer in the beginning of the year?

_____
_____
_____
_____
_____

3. How would you describe yourself as a writer now?

_____
_____
_____
_____
_____

4. Comment on how using a writer's notebook has helped you this year.

_____
_____
_____
_____

5. Include three notebook entries—one from the beginning, middle, and end of the year—to show your progress. On sticky notes, point out how your writing improves throughout the year.

6. What revision techniques have you found work best for you?

_____
_____
_____
_____
_____

Include a piece of finished writing that shows that you used one of the techniques mentioned above.

7. What have you learned about editing this year?

_____
_____
_____
_____
_____

8. As a writer, during which part of the process do you write best? Explain.

_____
_____
_____
_____
_____

9. Using the rubric, evaluate your writer's notebook below:

    Flexibility and Fluency: _____
    Thoughtfulness: _____
    Frequency: _____
    Overall Score: _____

Additional Comments:

10. Considering all of this information, what grade do you believe best describes your writing performance this fourth quarter? Explain your reasoning. Remember you will share this evaluation with me and together we'll determine your grade.

_____
_____
_____
_____
_____

References

Alvarez, Julia. 1999. *Something to Declare.* New York: Plume Books.

Anderson, Laurie. 2002. *Thank You, Sarah: The Woman Who Saved Thanksgiving.* New York: Simon and Schuster Children's Publishing.

Baylor, Byrd. 1995. *I'm in Charge of Celebrations.* New York: Aladdin Picture Books.

Bunting, Eve. 2001. *Gleam and Glow.* New York: Harcourt Children's Books.

Blume, Judy. 1995. *The Pain and the Great One.* New York: Yearling Books.

Bomer, Randy. 1995. *Time for Meaning: Crafting Literate Lives in Middle and High School.* Portsmouth, NH: Heinemann.

Bynum, Russ. September 18, 2004. "Amid Surging Water, Father Faced Wretched Decision." *Atlanta Journal-Constitution.*

Calkins, Lucy. 1988. *The Art of Teaching Writing.* Portsmouth, NH: Heinemann.

Cameron, Julia. 1992. *The Artist's Way.* New York: Jeremy P. Tarcher Books.

Catling, Patrick. 1995. *The Chocolate Touch.* New York: Yearling Books.

Clements, Andrew. 1998. *Frindle.* New York: Aladdin.

Creech, Sharon. 1996. *Walk Two Moons.* New York: HarperTrophy.

cummings, e. e. 2002. "maggie and milly and molly and may." In *95 Poems*. New York: Liveright Publishing.

Dakos, Kalli. 1992. *If You're Not Here, Please Raise Your Hand: Poems About School*. New York: The Trumpet Club.

DiCamillo, Kate. 2003. *The Tale of Despereaux*. Cambridge, MA: Candlewick Books.

Fletcher, Ralph. 1996a. *A Writer's Notebook: Unlocking the Writer Within You*. New York: HarperTrophy.

———. 1996b. *Breathing In, Breathing Out: Keeping a Writer's Notebook*. Portsmouth, NH: Heinemann.

———. 1996c. *Fig Pudding*. New York: Yearling Books.

———. 1997. *Twilight Comes Twice*. New York: Clarion Books.

Frank, Mitch. 2002. *Understanding September 11th*. New York: Viking Books.

Freedman, Russell. 1992. *Indian Chiefs*. New York: Holiday House.

Friedrich, Elizabeth. 1996. *Leah's Pony*. Honesdale, PA: Boyds Mills Press.

George, Kristine O'Connell. 1997. *The Great Frog Race*. New York: Clarion Books.

Graves, Donald. 2002. *Testing Is Not Teaching: What Should Count in Education*. Portsmouth, NH: Heinemann.

Harvey, Stephanie, and Anne Goudvis. 2000. *Strategies That Work: Teaching Comprehension to Enhance Understanding*. Portland, ME: Stenhouse Publishers.

Henkes, Kevin. 1996. *Chrysanthemum*. New York: HarperTrophy.

Hiaasen, Carl. 2002. *Hoot.* New York: Knopf Books for Young Readers.

Hindley, Joanne. 1996. *In the Company of Children.* Portland, ME: Stenhouse Publishers.

Hoose, Phillip, and Hannah Hoose. 1998. *Hey, Little Ant.* New York: Tricycle Books.

King, Stephen. 2002. *On Writing: A Memoir of the Craft.* New York: Pocket Books.

Klise, Kate. 2002. *Trial by Journal.* New York: HarperTrophy.

Krull, Kathleen. 2003. *Harvesting Hope: The Story of Cesar Chavez.* New York: Harcourt Children's Books.

Lamott, Anne. 1994. *Bird by Bird.* New York: Anchor Books.

Lester, Julius, and Jerry Pickney. 1999. *John Henry.* New York: Puffin Books.

Marzano, Robert J., Debra J. Pickering and Jane E. Pollock. 2001. *Classroom Instruction That Works: Research-Based Strategies for Increasing Student Achievement.* Alexandria, VA: Association for Supervision and Curriculum Development.

Miller, Debbie. 2002. *Reading with Meaning: Teaching Comprehension in the Primary Grades.* Portland, ME: Stenhouse Publishers.

Munson, Derek. 2000. *Enemy Pie.* New York: Chronicle Books.

Murphy, Jim. 1995. *The Great Fire.* New York: Scholastic.

Numeroff, Laura Joffe. 1991. *If You Give a Moose a Muffin.* New York: Laura Geringer Books.

Ray, Katie Wood. 1996. *Wondrous Words.* Urbana, IL: National Council of Teachers of English Press.

Schertle, Alice. 1996. *Keepers.* New York: HarperCollins.

Scieszka, Jon. 1995. *The True Story of the Three Little Pigs.* New York: Dutton.

Smith, Frank. 1996. *Reading Without Nonsense.* New York: Teachers College Press.

Spinelli, Jerry. 1999. *Maniac Magee.* New York: Little, Brown Publishers.

Weaver, Constance. 2002. *Reading Process and Practice.* 3d ed. Portsmouth, NH: Heinemann.

White, E. B. 1974. *Charlotte's Web.* New York: HarperTrophy.

Wiles, Deborah. 2002. *Love, Ruby Lavender.* New York: Gulliver Books Paperbacks.